MESSENGER
IN THE MIRROR

MESSENGER
IN THE MIRROR

Take back your power by understanding the patterns
and pay-offs in your key relationships, and learn how
to attract the love you deserve.

DYAN BELONJE

Published by Quickfox Publishing
PO Box 50660, West Beach, Bloubergrandt, 7441
Cape Town, South Africa
www.quickfox.co.za
info@quickfox.co.za

First edition 2009
Second edition 2018

Messenger in the Mirror
ISBN 978-0-620-43723-3

Copyright © Dyan Belonje

Edited by Rachel Bey-Miller
Proofread by Nina Gelderblom
Cover and book design by Vanessa Wilson
Typesetting and production by Quickfox Publishing

Cover photographs/artwork courtesy of
www.bigstockphoto.com (Johanna Goodyear; Kirsty Pargeter)

Also available as an ebook

CONTENTS

Let me make something clear here. You are all my messengers. Every one of you. You are all sending a message to life about life throughout your own life, lived. The question is not "are you a messenger?" The question is "what is the message you are sending?"

Excerpt from *Home with God* by Neale Donald Walsh

THANKS

To Mark for bringing me the message of love – and for
being my mirror.
To Riyan for being my messenger of hope – my ray
of light over many years.
Also to two special kindred spirits: Rachel, the editor and
Vanessa, the publisher – for your commitment and authenticity.
And to you – all of my messengers – for creating
opportunities for me to find myself.

*The most important questions in life can never be
answered by anyone except oneself.*

John Fowles

Before this book begins

Life presents us with obstacles for which there are no foolproof recipes
or ready-made answers, and most of us have found ourselves stuck in a
relationship, job, or situation with no clear way out. We know instinctively
that no one has the exact answers we're searching for ... what's more, we
suspect that those answers are locked up inside ourselves, but we don't
know how to access them. If only we could find the right questions ...

It is not the answer that enlightens, but the question.

Eugene Ionesco

As we pass through our lives, we cross paths with many messengers. These
are the people and the experiences that touch us on our journey. The
messages they bring can be found in something as simple as a fleeting
moment, or a connection spanning years, and we can choose whether
to take note of these messages or not. Some may cause us to weep as our
hearts break, and others to dance with joy as our hearts are filled. But all
the messages we receive will hold the clues to the questions we need to be
asking. And once we have formulated the questions, the answers begin to
flow into our consciousness of their own accord – if we wait a while and
let them.

From the moment your life begins here on earth, you are introduced
to your messengers. They are the people who parent you, they are your
friends and your colleagues, they are the insights you get from nature
and from your companion animals. Every experience tells you something
about yourself, but you need to be awake to hear it. When you become
involved in intimate relationships, your focus will be drawn to the
messages more clearly because that is where you place your attention. And

9

when you look into the relationship mirror, you may find that whatever you give out is being reflected back to you.

Every one of you will have felt the hurt at receiving an unwanted message from someone. These messages come packaged especially for you – they hold the clues to you finding yourself. What you need to do is sit with them, unwrap them, and look at them. Once you start doing this, you will be on your way to growing the way that you need to, and to finding the purpose and love you are looking for.

Messages can be transmitted in as many ways as they are received. Your response to the messages received depends on who gives you the message and how it is transmitted – you choose the effect it has on you. If someone says, "It's always about you, isn't it?" ... can you hear the *real* message instead of the criticism? "Something about me, in the way that I engage with the world, makes me seem selfish and uncaring. I need to do this differently because it's not a true reflection of who I am."

It is important that you don't become enmeshed in the drama because nothing will be resolved and your path to the next level will be blocked. You will stay tied up in the same web with the same issues. Do you find yourself creating the same patterns in your relationships? Do they all look the same, only the people are different? The ways in which you relate will repeat over and over until you get the message.

This book takes you on a journey to discover how you came to think, feel and respond in the way that you do, and to help you uncover and shed light on what's really happening. And to do that, it will pose many questions. Take note of the questions that resonate with you most – these will hold the seeds of the answers you need in your specific situation. You will also find guidance in unpacking the messages and using them to develop a closer relationship with yourself and with others. And ultimately, you will discover that what you do to another, you do also to yourself.

BEING WHO WE ARE

꩜

*I bring you the message of uniqueness ... to listen to your inner voice.
You will be reminded of who you really are.*

꩜

What are the colours of your thoughts as the messenger drops the message into your heart and breaks it? How many pieces of yourself did you lose to this messenger when you were together and how will you fill the emptiness now that you are apart? Can you quietly smile at your reflection in the shop window as the message you've received unfolds, and do you say, "I am still worthy"? Can you accept this lesson with an abundant spirit of humility, or is it easier for you to cling to the hand of fear and walk in darkness?

Protection programming

We all have choice; we have free will. And yet we choose to sabotage ourselves by becoming hypnotically enslaved by our fear-programming, both from our environment and from our genes. The programs that run our lives are set up by us through our experiences and, most often, we do not even realise we are using them. They are the default routes that we follow when we feel unsafe, the habits in which we take comfort and the things that we do to ourselves to avoid confronting our pain.

If a current situation pushes a button that reminds you of an unpleasant past experience, you may revert to your *protection program* to avoid repeating the negative experience. So instead of stepping out of your comfort zone and expressing your truth, you retreat to your uncomfortable, familiar place because it is predictable and you believe it is under your control. You have seen it before and you know what it looks like.

And in denying the truth of your feelings, you damage the potential of your expansive possibility because, by not daring to venture even a glimpse of what you may really look like, you miss out on the opportunity of recognising your real power, of seeing who you really are.

You prefer to guard yourself with a known routine, your usual numbness…day after day after day. An alarm wakes you up and you think to yourself as you drink your first cup of coffee, "Is it only Wednesday?" And you count the days to Friday or pay-day or your holiday. You consider how much fun you will have then and what a meaningless existence this is really – working to live and living to work. As you drive off in your car you watch all the others scurrying around with tired eyes and something deep within you whispers, "There is more to life than this, you know…".

The shapes we're in

Each of us has an equal opportunity to express and define our personal uniqueness. We are not the same as one another and we were never meant to be clones of each other. However, we all yearn for the same thing. We spend much of our lives chasing a feeling – the best feeling that we can have. We want to love and feel loved, and we follow different paths in search of this, and find different means of achieving it.

Each one of us has the potential for success, but not necessarily within the frameword that we were trained to define ourselves. If you look around you, what messages do you receive from society? Do you notice how important status and materialism are made out to be? And yet we keep hearing that money cannot buy us love. Why do we then buy into this illusion and aspire to climb the ladder to loneliness? Is this really achieving success?

Take an objective view of the messages in this world and you will notice how we are being sold products in exchange for popularity and acceptance. You will feel worthy and acknowledged only if you wear this perfume; cook this meal; drive this car; and own this label. Why? Because you will be receiving the attention and admiration of others – and this makes you feel good.

There is nothing that you *have* to do in this life. We do what we *choose* to do, and we are led by the circumstantial decisions that support our priorities at the time. Often we get sucked into society's vortex; we do what we think is expected of us and we forget how to *be*, because we forget who we are.

But, we all carry the energy of our ancestors and the yearning of our souls, and that is why we have moments in which we are reminded of our perfect paradise, of something more. And yet we are always in search of a magical potion that will soothe our vacant spaces, fulfil our being, and wake us up. However, the key lies within us – it is not out there hiding in some elusive experience – and that is why we overlook it. There is a beautiful Hindi legend in which Brahman, the Supreme Being, after creating the world, said to the Angels, "Where shall I hide now that my work is done?" And they answered, "In the hearts of men and women because no-one will think to look for you there."

We spend so much of our time searching that we forget to stop and see the self within ourselves, for ourselves. We allow others to define us and affirm our being so that we do not feel invisible. We want to be acknowledged, to be seen and appreciated for who we are; but if we do not see ourselves, how can others? Yet we give others the power to grant us permission to breathe. And we dare not sit still long enough to hear our thoughts and enjoy our own company for fear that we will be labelled unproductive and unworthy. Being busy means we are useful, and being useful means we are needed, which means we've earned our place and we can stay.

Sadly, we become addicted to the possibility of someone else or something else 'finding us' and them or it filling the void and making us feel transiently whole. We run aimlessly in circles around ourselves and although we are essentially going nowhere, the movement and the fatigue indicate that there is direction. We allow ourselves to become desperately dependent beings, ignorant of our independent yet interconnected souls. The perfect simplicity of everything being within us and within our reach is neglected because it appears too easy and we are taught that life is meant to be hard. We are injected with earthly definitions of how complicated life is; that we all have a cross to bear. And we forget the simple laws of Spiritual intelligence – especially the law that says: *Know thyself.*

Themes and threads

Throughout our lives we weave patterns and connections with others. They form part of the human system in which we relate and learn and live. Some of our contacts are meaningful, others less so, but we all have some sort of reciprocal effect on one another. It's not the duration of our interactions that makes them memorable, but the quality or impact that we feel when we are part of them. And sometimes, it's not what people *say*, but how they *are* that changes us. Their presence is the catalyst for our change.

It is important to look at the themes and patterns that we weave in our relationships. Do we relate to our family members in the same way we relate to friends, colleagues and our life partners? Do you find yourself re-creating the same communication errors, the same conversations, the same arguments – just with different people? It is a very obvious statement, but if you do what you always did, you can only get what you always got. Your relationship with yourself will determine how willing you are to share of yourself; of how comfortably you can be a part of the social weave of relationships, yet still retain your individual identity.

What are the common factors in all your relationships? Why do you keep shooting the messenger when the message remains the same? This is as futile as squashing all the worms and wondering why there are no butterflies.

Do you feel misunderstood in your relationships? And how much of yourself are you willing – or forced – to reveal? Are you really authentic in how you relate to others, or do you hold back parts of yourself for fear of showing your heart? Ironically, hiding your truth from others is as detrimental to yourself and others as hiding it from yourself – you can only be totally understood if you are true to yourself and are willing to put all your inside information *out there*. Secrets create disharmony, misunderstandings and distrust. How uncomfortable do you feel allowing yourself to be transparent by communicating with honesty?

When you allow someone to see through you – into your secret spaces and your vulnerabilities – your fears and anxieties lose their power. Keeping them in the dark gives them the opportunity to breed and grow and become monsters that ultimately turn to feed on you.

Generally, we can perpetuate unhealthy patterns until they stop working for us. We can choose to stay stuck in what we know to avoid the unfamiliarity of the unknown, as well as to, perhaps, satisfy the need to keep a fantasy relationship alive. It is easier to dream it than live it; or so we think.

One of the biggest mistakes we continue to make is thinking that someone will change and become what we want them to be because we are now in a relationship with them. No-one intrinsically changes in a relationship. We simply have different facets of ourselves enhanced or diminished by the new interaction with the next person. Depending on the pay-off and the feeling that this gives us, we will either maintain or discard our new behavioural expression. In other words, if you find yourself behaving in a different way in a new relationship and this change makes you feel good, the chances are high that you will carry on doing more of the same because the reward or pay-off that you receive makes it worthwhile.

Therefore, through our relationships with others in the world, we are shaped and moulded into who and what we are. Our entire holistic expression – our karma, our lessons, and our soul searching for expression – is what we offer to our interactions. The environment and the people who form part of our circumstance provide us with the opportunity to co-create our space on earth. Generally we all want the same thing, and we try our best with what we have learned, to find the greatest feeling that we can.

But how do we deconstruct unhealthy relationship patterns? And can we really take ourselves apart and rebuild ourselves, without falling to pieces?

WHERE WE BEGIN

❧

*I bring you the message of choice … reminding you
of your decision to enter this lifetime, and of the people
you chose as a means of getting here.*

❧

Family is usually our earliest experience of interrelating with other people. These people are the ones who inculcate and enculturate us with the norms and values known to them. They can only teach us what they have learned, and in the way that they understand. They will pass on their lessons and their issues to us; their strengths and their weaknesses.

There is a Jesuit saying, "Give me the child until he is seven and I will give you the man." This is how important those first few formative years are to our development. They lay down the wiring and the networks that determine our ability to engage in the world as adults.

What the academics say

When we are *in utero* and thereafter when we enter the world, whatever and whoever surrounds us will be stored as new information on our clean slate; as something to mimic and something to remember. The Behavioural Theorists proposed the idea that if our behaviour is positively reinforced, more of the same behaviour will be encouraged. Therefore, if one accepts the principle that we will adapt our behaviour to achieve the highest pay-off or the most rewarding feeling, or whatever it is that creates the best possible solution or sensation, it follows that behaviour creating a positive outcome will be stored as useful behaviour. In the same way, behaviour that creates a negative outcome will be rejected or repressed.

In this way we do tend to behave very much like circus animals. We are trained by our environment and we are conditioned by our experiences. Generally, we will move away from a negative stimulus and gravitate towards a positive one. But, because we are all programmed differently, our definitions of aversive experiences and pleasant stimuli will not be the same.

We should not be surprised then if children – who are exposed mainly to TV and computer games – grow up believing that this is how one engages with the world. Their reality will include aspiring to 'Bold and Beautiful' relationships and they will learn that conflict resolution can be attained through games in which blowing someone else's head off gives you extra points.

The Social Learning theorists believe that there is a thinking process that accompanies our learning and that we are not merely trained and conditioned. In other words, active role playing involving both the body and the mind takes place.

The Person Oriented Approach supports the concept that it is the responsibility of the individual to fully experience life. We, as individuals, make rational decisions and are not at the mercy of the environment or our unconscious drives. It is we who influence our personal growth and make the choices about how we can increase our self awareness and more fully experience our reality. We direct our own lives and strive for optimum development.

But, what if the rational choices that we make to direct our lives are subtly influenced by the patterns that have been silently laid down over time? We may think that we are making our own choices, but all we are doing is behaving in response to environmental cues and learned programming.

How do we learn to feel and have pleasure, and not fear happiness? And integrate acceptance of ourselves with unconditional acceptance of others? How do we merge into a world that has been polarized into good and bad, black and white... and feel the colours in the greyness?

Family trees

We inherit genetic possibilities from both our parents and this information codes for the possibility to build ourselves up or to break ourselves down. The environment in which we live determines whether certain programming is activated to affect us positively or negatively, or whether it lies dormant. The natural genetic helix in our cells senses the environment and can be awakened by different experiences. What we feel in our body will result in us creating thoughts and then these thoughts will decide how we should act. We will choose behaviour that we feel is best for us in the situation in which we find ourselves.

Each person is unique and therefore one can neither generalise nor apply a single formula to suit all people. If someone has the genetic predisposition to behave in a certain way, this temperament trait requires the right triggers in the environment to be switched on and activated. We live and learn – and we learn to live.

Therefore, because we inherit the template of our ancestors and we are raised in the environment of our parents, we will learn from them what they perceive to be safe and familiar. This is the soup in which we are immersed from the day we are conceived – and the very first images that we have of our new world are seen in this family space.

This environment also provides us with the experiences we need in order to find our own unique paths – paths that are designed for our greatest good.

Time frames

There are many theories on the stages of human development, which are all written by people who were and still are influenced by their subjective experiences and their particular field of interest. Theories are not derived in isolation – the people writing them form part of a social structure that shapes and moulds their thought processes. Because everyone's view of the same incident is different, gathering as many snapshots as possible of the same situation enables us to form a more complete picture.

The first year

Sigmund Freud, the father of psychoanalysis, termed the first year of life the *oral phase* because the child has both the need for nutrition and the need for pleasure that is satisfied through sucking the mother's breast. During this act, the baby has the mother's full attention and nurturance. Some babies may enjoy this phase so much that they could experience the transition to the next phase as a threat. They may continue desiring oral objects and will resort to sucking a dummy or their thumbs to compensate for their loss, as well as to pacify the perceived rejection they feel. According to Freud, if an individual remains fixed or partially fixated at this phase, they may grow into a very dependent adult who displays characteristics of narcissism and excessive optimism, and perhaps a tendency to be jealous and envious of others.

Erik Erikson viewed the first year of life as being critical to the development of trust in a threatening world. He cited the child's relationship with its mother as being of primary importance in this developmental phase. During our first year, we develop the concept of hope by establishing a healthy balance between trust and mistrust. In order to reach this point of synthesis, there needs to be a positive interaction between genetic and social influences. Our nature needs to be nurtured. This phase of our lives lays the foundation for how we will respond as adults to the question, "how far do you trust your environment to provide you with what you need?" Those who cannot trust this concept or do not understand the infinite abundance of the universe will tend to hoard things through fear of being without support. The absence of maternal support as an infant is then transferred to a need for material support later on in life. Do you find yourself saving things for a rainy day – a day that never materialises?

The second year

Our second year of life was described by Freud as the *anal phase*. According to his theory, children at this stage of development derive pleasure through excretion and retention. The parents take on the role of representing society and these societal rules reach the child via toilet training. Children also learn to use this function to punish their parents – for example by defying these rules in an act of inappropriate excretion or a refusal to go to the toilet. Toilet training is believed to have a profound effect on how an individual relates to orderliness and thriftiness later on in life.

Freud believed that an event causing emotional insecurity at this time can result in an obsessive compulsive personality type. Insecurity in our second year can turn us into an anally-retentive character with an unrealistic need to control our environment. Reflect on your home life when you were about two years old. Was there emotional trauma happening around you? What were the levels of emotional insecurity of your primary caregiver (usually your mother) at the time? If she was experiencing insecurities – such as the loss of her partner through death or rejection, for example – you will have taken on these insecurities. You would have felt her instability and stored it as yours. In your adult life, you may have an irrational need to control your environment; to establish some sort of order that is under your control.

Erikson defined this second phase as a dynamic conflict between freedom and discipline. This is the time during which we develop our willpower by creating a healthy synthesis between willful autonomy and the shame and doubt we may experience as a result of our failures. It is important that our self-confidence is not shattered through criticism of our shortfalls, and children at this stage should be encouraged to stand on their own two feet within the safety of an encouraging environment. This stage lays the foundation for the concepts of co-operation and wilfulness, freedom of self-expression and its suppression. Consider, for example, the use of phrases such as No!... Don't touch... You can't... Stop that... Bad boy... Stupid girl. These continual military-like orders can result in someone feeling doubtful about their abilities and it makes exploration almost impossible. Their spirit of adventure is crushed, self determination is lost, and self-esteem is sought through an external source. Everything feels impossible. "It cannot be done. I can't stand up for myself. I will wait for instruction from someone else because I am bad and stupid. I am not worthy of making my own decisions."

Children in their third year of life are often referred to as being in the 'terrible twos' stage. This is a time of transition from a trusting baby into a stubborn little person. At this stage it is vitally important to separate the behaviour from the child when reprimanding the child for bad behaviour: "I love you, but your behaviour is bad," instead of, "you are bad." What is needed is unconditional acceptance of their individuality, within a structure that supports who they are and shows them where they belong.

Social Learning theorists emphasise the importance of the interaction between the person, the situation, and the behaviour that occurs within a particular situation. The unique combination of these three ingredients affects the situation, and the new situation in turn affects the behaviour, and so on. It is a constant reciprocal dance on the wheel of life. We think about and interpret stimuli we receive, and make assumptions about what we could expect to happen when we decide to behave in a certain way. We learn to self regulate through our ongoing interactions with the environment, and the reflections and shadows that are mirrored back at us.

Wire-monkey mothers

A *wire-monkey-mother* raises badly socialised individuals who find being cared for a foreign concept. These individuals know only rejection and emotional neglect and as a result, are usually drawn to unhealthy partnerships as adults.

Harry Harlow (Harlow, 1958) proved this concept by using two surrogate wire mothers for baby monkeys, one of which was covered with a soft cloth. Each baby monkey had a feeding bottle for food and a light bulb to provide warmth. The baby monkeys showed a distinct preference for the cloth mother rather than the wire monkey mother in all instances, whether it be hunger, fear or the need for comforting. However, Harlow noticed over time that these maternally deprived monkeys did not develop normal social and sexual behaviour, and when they grew up, they were unable to mate. If they were exposed to fear-provoking situations, they displayed signs of seriously insecure behaviour by clutching themselves, rocking backwards and forwards, and making screeching sounds. Monkeys who had a 'safe base' – a nurturing mother to scamper back to when they felt the need for comfort – were more inquisitive and playful.

The conclusion Harlow came to was that, besides warmth, food and softness, the baby monkeys also needed social interaction for normal social development. Therefore, if a child is born to a wire-monkey mother, this child will not be shown how to relate in a nurturing manner and will not recognize it in later years when he or she starts to form intimate relationships. Cold, uncaring, non-committal relationships will be familiar to these individuals, whereas caring and warm interactions will be regarded with suspicion. These studies also revealed that touch is more critical than any other form of contact in mother-infant bonding. Non-nurtured children often transform into adolescents who will do anything for love because they are desperate to be held and comforted. The danger of this desperate need is that it often leads to indiscriminate sex and/or substance abuse because these individuals have no idea what they are looking for or how to fill the void they continue to feel.

3 to 6 years

Freud called the developmental stage between 3-6 years old the *phallic phase* as the male sexual organ forms the central theme of this stage. Freud postulated that the boy-child feels jealous of his father's place in his mother's life and wants to replace him. The child then deals with this Oedipus Complex by identifying with his father, by imitating him, and by absorbing and accepting his father's moral rules as his own. If the father is too strict at this phase, the child may internalize the father's strict rules and may not learn to express anger outward towards his father. This aggression will then be directed internally against himself.

This behaviour is reinforced if a child is exposed to a hostile home environment and is punished for expressing his feelings. These children will feel that it is not OK to make a mistake. They develop a heightened awareness of the emotions of others and they discard their own feelings because they do not trust them anymore. These children feel responsible for the anger of their parents and they start to toe the line as a solution to their survival. *Tell me what I am supposed to do because obedience equals life.*

A child who gets attention from adults by acting out certain behaviours will continue to act this way if the attention received is processed as pleasurable and desirable. If someone's behaviour continues to be positively reinforced, acting out will become a way of being later in life. This behaviour becomes a means of getting the desired attention, which ultimately provides the necessary validation from the relevant others in that person's life. Their self-worth will be intertwined with, and determined by, the reactions of others. *I entertain other people; therefore I'm worthy and acceptable.*

Therefore, if you notice an adult with attention-seeking behaviour, you can be sure that they gained attention this way as a child. They feel insecure if they are not the centre of attention. It is just too uncomfortable. They forget that they have grown up now and are likely to continue to tell the same jokes and love being the party animal.

In girl-children this phase is often referred to as the time when she develops the female Oedipus Complex (termed the Electra Complex by Jung). During this stage of her psycho-sexual development she has an unconscious romantic desire for her father and becomes hostile and envious towards her mother in an attempt to get his attention. This desire fades as she realises that she will never 'possess' her father.

If this complex remains unresolved and the girl-child receives inadequate or inappropriate attention from her father, she may later develop what is often referred to as 'daddy issues'. She may look for male approval elsewhere and usually in a sexual manner. Females with unresolved daddy issues may be drawn to relationships with older men (a father figure), or they may re-create their bad relationships with their fathers by choosing abusive relationships.

Adolescence

Adolescence marks the time when the greatest degree of identity development occurs. Erikson focussed quite extensively on adolescence and the identity crisis that occurs at this stage of our lives. He said that during this stage of our development we develop a feeling of having an identity and that this feeling has three components:

- being certain about which group you belong to in society – having a social identity,
- being sure of who you are, and
- knowing what your personal values and ideals are.

In other words, as adolescents we should be able to answer the following questions: Who am I? To which group do I belong? What would I like to achieve? Erikson's theory maintains that once we have experimented with different roles and are able to make a commitment to one role, we will know who we are and we will also be aware of other possible identity choices that we could have made. It is therefore a critical time for the formation of our identity – of how comfortable we feel being who we are.

Did you have loving validation of who you were during your formative years? Did you receive unconditional positive regard for who you were, or were you defined by your behaviour? If you processed the information, 'any attention is better than no attention,' you have to be aware that you may have incorrectly wired yourself to believe that pain – or any other unhealthy attention – equals love.

We can anaesthetise ourselves enough to block out what we find fearful and neglectful, but this eventually leads to a sensation of confusion because our behaviour was conditioned through double-bind parenting – "Come here … I hate you."

If you were not trained to feel emotions in a healthy and appropriate way, this energy-sensation becomes difficult to express because you have not been taught how to feel emotion. This can result in the polarisation of expressions because there is no balance or consistency in expressing emotion. One week you may experience an intense focus on the need for something spiritual and the next week your pendulum swings and you are driven to a need for self-destructive sex and substance abuse. You sit on a see-saw that fluctuates between light and dark because your heart is closed. The only way this inconsistent energy can be released is through love – self love and the love of humanity. How do you express love? Is your heart centre open and do you know what it feels like? Is it possible to feel love when you are constantly riding a roller coaster?

Parenting styles

Parents train their children through varying parenting styles. Baumrind (1971) identified three main parenting styles: authoritarian, authoritative and permissive. Maccoby and Martin (1983) added a fourth one, the uninvolved parenting style.

The authoritarian parent

Authoritarian parents expect their children to obey them under all circumstances – no questions asked. If children do not conform to their parents' wishes, they are punished. These children often grow up with a relatively low self-esteem and also have difficulty in relating to their friends. Some may be inclined to engage in antisocial behaviour, searching for 'safer' avenues to vent their feelings of anger and fear, which they are unable to express in their punitive home environment. Examples of this would be expressing anger through graffiti or vandalising property, as well as being involved in theft and/or by being deceitful.

The authoritative parent

Authoritative parents allow their children freedom within reasonable rules. They show patience and sensitivity and allow their children to contribute to family discussions. These children grow up with a high self-esteem and are generally more independent, and more willing to try new things, than other children.

The permissive parent

Permissive or indulgent parents exercise very little control over their children and as a result the children are able to do as they please. These children are generally seen as lacking in self-control, are reluctant to accept responsibility, and often demonstrate a less mature attitude when socialising with their friends at school.

The uninvolved parent

Uninvolved parents are detached and indifferent. They supply the basic needs such as food and clothing, but do not make any effort to spend time with their children. As a result, these children are generally more impulsive than their peers, and often engage in antisocial behaviour.

Birth order

Another very relevant and important influence on behaviour is the order in which the siblings in a family are born. Alfred Adler raised attention to the fact that children of the same family are not raised in the same environment. The oldest child is initially the only child and receives all the possible attention. When the second child arrives, the first child has to share this attention with another. The oldest child strives to stay ahead and to maintain something of what he or she was accustomed to, whereas the second child is constantly 'in training' in an attempt to overtake the first child.

The youngest child often goes their own way and creates a life that differs from that of the other family members. The arrival of a third child puts the second child in the middle. These middle children often feel squeezed out. Middle children may, in some cases, express a 'woe is me' attitude. This early childhood training and the learned personality trends of interrelating within the hierarchical birth order shapes how people interact with others as adults.

Hostility at home

If you were raised in a tense and hostile household environment, you are likely to be someone who is hypersensitive to the possibility of 'danger'. You were raised to be constantly on the alert and will probably be extremely quick learning new behaviours. You become wary of danger (real and perceived threats) more quickly than those raised in a safer home environment.

Survivors of childhood hostility and emotional neglect may suffer from residual post traumatic stress disorder (PTSD). They may instinctively

27

run from relationships because they perceive a certain type of behaviour or a word as life-threatening, especially in a circumstance in which they are sharing space with another. Any cue (a word or an action) that they have learned during their growing years to be a sign of danger will result in an intense need to escape. "I've got to get out of here", will be their top-of-mind thought.

People from these unsafe homes are also able to read subtle meta-communication very well and they sense someone's body language long before, and much more accurately, than those raised in a safer environment. These individuals are sometimes seen as 'psychic' because they developed a heightened sense of awareness and intuition as a survival tool during childhood. These individuals often feel safer living in their created – or imaginary – world than in their real environment. They learned to trust angels and fairies more than people.

What is good for you? Can you safely share space with others, or do you need your own safety zone? When do you feel safe and when do you feel threatened? What is your comfort zone of familiarity? But remember – what is comfortable is not always right or healthy.

What are emotions?

Antonio Damasio defined the term *emotional state* as a collection of responses between parts of the brain and the body, as well as between various part of the brain. As we go through life, we learn to pair emotion with facts. This pairing is held in our memory so that we can reactivate the paired emotion (or an aspect of it) when a similar situation arises in us. That is what we refer to when we say we have a 'gut feeling'. Damasio describes the term *feeling* as, *the complex mental state that results from the emotional state.* Feelings are how we experience our emotional state – in other words, how we experience the feedback from our bodies.

So we learn through our circumstances about what serves us well and what does not. Emotions become coupled with events and are remembered as pleasant or unpleasant. If we find ourselves continually revisiting what we consider to be an unpleasant circumstance, our *pay-off* programming needs to be investigated. Why do we deliberately choose to sabotage ourselves? What are we getting out of it (the pay-off)?

And love? Some say that it is a feeling of completion – when you want nothing and hold on to nothing. When your soul forms the fragile connection with its purity of truth, and you are touched by the pulse of creation. And once you have felt this, you are able to love another and will feel the stillness within them as your own. You will be able to honour the role that they play in your life – both as your teacher and as your student.

Namaste
I honour the place in you in which the entire universe dwells.
I honour the place in you which is of love, of truth, of light,
and of peace. When you are in that place within you, and I am
in that place within me, then we are one.

Our environment

We must realise that our environment is neither good nor bad – until we try to control it. Environments are also neither neutral nor are they static. They are shifting mercurial jesters that carve and mould us and provide us with the backdrop against which to act out our deepest fears and our highest hopes. They are the arena over which we have no control and with which we are intimately intertwined. The harder we try to control what is happening around us, the more weathered and tired we become because we are futilely fighting the relentless storms and buffeting winds that surround us.

Only those who live in fear are out of control of themselves and so need to control their surroundings – including the need to control the people within that environment. Why do we not learn to play with the wind and ride the power of the storm? The more we trust the things that are powerful and empowering within ourselves and the more we aspire to holding our own stillness in the storm, the more open our eyes will be to see the promises that rainbows bring.

But – through our inflexibility – we crack, because the pressure of controlling the system becomes too intense. Not everyone cracks in the same way, and each one of us has a unique manner of displaying our desperation. Where do you go to neutralise the tension of being a control-freak? Where is the place that you run to – to feel safely *out-of-control?*

Individuals experience the same environment differently because we all perceive circumstances according to our personal frame of reference. Our reactions are based on what we have learned. The behaviour and interpretation that follows is an extension of what has served us best in the past. We instinctively default to what we perceive to be the best option: What is the best pay-off for me? How do I need to behave to avoid feeling punished and/or rejected? This may not – realistically – be the ideal way of behaving or engaging in the world, but it is the way that we have subjectively decided will produce the best possible outcome for us.

We are inherently drawn to that which is familiar because we think it is safer. We know what it looks like. It is what we have practiced over and over and therefore we know it best because we have the experience. Little do we realise that the familiar is actually a furry monster that we feed and keep alive, which then turns around and bites us.

What is it that you do to get the sensation that you define as 'good'? The early recollections we have of childhood times never leave us. Sometimes we choose to forget; sometimes we forget to remember. But they are always there and will rise to muddy the waters or soothe the ripples of our lives. It just depends on where in the pond you are catching your thoughts.

THE PHYSICAL BODY

ↂ

I bring you the message of awareness… to listen to your body.
You will be reminded of how you are treating yourself.

ↂ

Disease is what we experience in our body when we are out of alignment with ourselves. But when and why does this happen? Conventional thinking dictates that we look to organic causes for our ailments and to solve our problems. Usually we will consult a medical doctor who will conduct a physical examination to determine whether there is any evidence of a bacterial, parasitic or viral infection – or perhaps address an obvious injury or investigate something less overt such as a genetic ailment. If no obvious organic cause can be found, you may be labeled 'burnt-out'. If you happen to read the medical notes, you will see the phrase, "The patient has an idiopathic disorder". This basically means that you have a physical ailment arising from an unknown cause. But – if you have been labeled 'stressed' or 'burnt out' and you are feeling unwell – where does this feeling come from and why is it stuck in your body?

Understanding the 'system'

We have been debating the connection between the physical and mental aspects of ourselves for centuries. One particular approach that arose to explain this connection is called *dualism*.

31

Dualism suggests that there are two kinds of existence – namely, a mental world and a physical world.

René Descartes (1596–1650) believed that two separate events – the mental (mind) and physical (body) – interact and the mind produces an effect on the body. For example, if your mental world is filled with worry over having too much debt, your physical body may respond by developing high blood pressure – and when you start worrying about your high blood pressure, your heart will beat faster and you may end up having a heart attack. In other words, there appears to be a relationship between these two entities. Our mind has an influence on our body; mind over matter.

In more recent times, science has discovered that everything we are forms part of a greater whole, and everything we do affects the whole. Our bodies are a complete system within themselves, and each individual part has an influence on the entire system. Our bodies have complex feedback loops whereby information from the body is felt by the mind and vice versa.

Not only are we, as individuals, made up of systems, but we also form part of a unit called the family system, which forms part of the community, which makes up the nation … and ultimately, the living beings of the world. If we are part of a dysfunctional family, we too will be dysfunctional in some way, because the symptoms that we have will be supported and maintained by our family system. To change one dysfunctional member means that a change to the identity of the entire system must occur. In the same way, the 'family' of our component parts (mental, physical, emotional and spiritual aspects) that make up our individual identity all have a reciprocal effect on each other and we are only as strong as our weakest component.

The body-mind connection

How do our physical forms express the emotional discomfort we experience? If we consider our bodies to be a barometer of what we're experiencing, we may start noticing the extent to which unhappiness with our lives and our relationships is evident in our bodies. One of the most obvious examples is when you feel physically ill or nauseaus at the thought of going home to an angry or abusive partner; the thought triggers an unpleasant emotion, and the unpleasant emotion triggers a physical response in the body. A less obvious example would be one in which, for instance, you develop an ear infection for no apparent reason; however, on review of your work environment, you realise that your boss has been verbally dumping on you non-stop over the past few months to the point where you just don't want to hear any more – your ears literally 'act out'.

Therefore, by becoming more in tune with ourselves, we will become more efficient at reading the subtle language of our bodies. This will give us more insight into what is happening in our thoughts.

How we choose our words can also provide us with many a clue. If you listen carefully to what someone says, you may find out what is lying beneath their apparently calm exterior, for instance:

"I have laryngitis again…"

"What are you trying to say? I can't hear you. Speak up!"

"I can't."

It's her larynx and vocal chords that have been affected, so perhaps her body is telling her that she has not been speaking out enough? It would benefit her to self-reflect and ask: "What is it that I need to express?", or "What is it that I fear talking about? Why can I not speak my truth?"

The more aware we are of the fact that our bodies are sending us messages, the more in touch with ourselves we will become. And when we notice those messages in others, we will be able to understand them just the same because we will have seen their behaviour in ourselves.

When we are ill, others are affected as we are affected by them; we are capable of infecting one another – not only physically, but sometimes just by how we are feeling. In a recent study, scientists at Stony Brook University in New York investigated the presence of certain signals that are released in the sweat of those who are experiencing fear. When we are exposed to these chemicals, we subconsciously smell the fear signals and our brains tell us that there is fear in the air. It seems to be contagious. However, there are also studies that have shown that happiness is contagious too! In other words, we absorb what others are feeling. We also know innately that we are capable of healing others, just by how we behave in our interactions with them.

Relationship partners often develop similar or the same physical manifestations as one another because we tend to act out our deepest psychological fear-issues on each other when we become emotionally vulnerable. This behaviour then triggers our sensitive weak-spots. Partners may share common insecurities and these could well have been why they were drawn to each other in the first place; they shared an intangible understanding, somehow seeing themselves mirrored in each other's vulnerability.

Even if we consistently ignore and store our unresolved issues, they will not disappear because they form part of what we have created; they are the side-effects of our actions and experiences. In an attempt to get our attention, these unresolved issues will gnaw away at our emotions – causing us to lose our balance – until, eventually, we become the issue and our physical body begins to show the cracks. Only then do we sit up and take note. At this point, we will give our neglected issues all of our attention because we are feeling disabled by them, and as a consequence we become associated with our personal 'dis-ease'. You may even recognise your own unresolved issues in the following scenario:

"Have you seen Barry lately?" she asked. "You must remember Bad-Back-Barry?"

"Oh yes! I do. He's still the same…taking on way too much responsibility. He was out of action again this weekend. His back seems to have gotten so much worse since he accepted that new position in the company."

The main reasons that we become stressed and ill are:

• we do not feel that we have the strength to hold down and fulfill our responsibilities,
• we think that we are not good enough being who we are – we lack self-worth and a belief in our abilities, and
• we procrastinate.

Caroline Myss discusses the concept of how our 'biography becomes our biology' in her book *Anatomy of the Spirit*. She makes us aware that if we hold onto negative attitudes, thoughts and memories, all the events associated with these become our baggage, as it did with Barry in the example. His back gave in under the strain of his feeling pressurised. He lost confidence in his abilities, which left him feeling vulnerable and unsupported (the back is linked with issues of support). And in an attempt to prove his value and self-worth, he took on even more work which only made his back problem worse.

Awareness

Have you ever noticed someone and thought that he or she looks *emotionally emaciated*? They come across as unnurtured and touch deprived. Without knowing or speaking to this person, you will recognise their emotional circumstance. The more our awareness grows, the more obvious other people's issues will be to us, because we start intuitively reading another's situation when we are in their presence. Because – through our greater awareness – we are more free to decentralise from our own circumstance to see the bigger picture. We move from being egocentric to being more inclusive and through our growth, we develop a healthy awareness of the reciprocal effect we have on others. However, with this conscious awareness comes the choice of becoming involved in the problems of others. Realistically, if someone wants you to share their problem, they should come to you at least twice before you decide to help them. Often people just want to dump their garbage on your doorstep; they do not really expect you to offer a solution.

We should remember that everyone has the right to be where they are in terms of their level of awareness and how they express their awareness, and that we have no right to interfere. This is what we term *conscious awareness* – with this consciousness comes the choice of becoming involved in the problems of others, or not. This concept of detached involvement is an interesting paradox, and TS Eliot worded it so perfectly when he wrote: *Teach us to care and not to care; teach us to sit still.* No-one can raise another's consciousness if they are not ready and willing. We can, however, focus on opportunities to raise our own consciousness. We can pay attention to the quality of our thoughts and keep them light so that they move us effortlessly up to the next level of awareness.

Have you ever heard yourself say to someone, "You make me sick"? This statement is usually a very accurate and prophetic one, as you may find that sharing your company with certain people can be nauseating and energy depleting. You may even feel repelled by their presence, both mentally and physically. Unfortunately, most often we choose to override our initial gut-feeling because we do not want to appear judgemental and so we hear others saying, "Give him a chance, don't be so unfair ... he's not so bad." If only we could learn to be fair on ourselves and listen to our bodies in the first thirty seconds of meeting someone; we would avoid becoming enmeshed with people who encourage our bad habits and in whose company we neglect our relationship with ourselves.

However, some would say that these are the very people we should be around because they bring with them a message. The emotional charge that we have when we meet them signals this. If we interact with them with a willingness to hear what they have to say, we will learn a great deal about who we are – even if our final thought is *I am not that*. If we take notice of the initial inner warning, we can have many life-enhancing experiences without becoming stuck on the hook. Not every interaction needs to develop into a sexual or love relationship.

Do you find yourself going back for more by socialising with people you know are not good for you? If someone calls you and demands to see you – as you hear their voice you remember that on every occasion that you have spent time with them you were left feeling drained, then why can you not say "no" to their invitation? Are you looking for something that is not there, or do you live in hope of them reaching what you deem to be their full potential? We have all experienced what it is like when an 'energy vampire' sucks the life out of us; refuelling their energy at our expense. But we have to realise that they do so because they can. Once you work out who the energy vampires are in your life, pay attention to why this is happening and then make a conscious decision to avoid them. If you keep being sucked in, ask yourself why you seem to need this form of abuse. Do you feel more worthy after giving someone else your self-worth and your energy? Is it easier for you to process other people's problems than to deal with your own?

Giving our power away

We generally do not like to admit to being a victim, yet we often display behaviour that indicates that we are feeling disempowered, out of control, or ignored; that we are slipping into victim consciousness. And it is not always that obvious. Consider the example where we hear someone say, "She always drains me, so she owes me. I've paid my dues. It's not my fault." However, if we dig a bit deeper, we find that this person has a pay-off for letting herself be drained by her energy vampire friend; she no longer feels ignored and invisible, she feels useful! Her victim consciousness mantra might be, "As long as you are in the wrong, I'm OK and you can pay. It's all your fault. What about me ...?"

Unfortunately, nothing is solved by playing these games; by getting a good feeling out of gaining a 'win' over a 'victim feeling'. Your anger remains, and because anger is toxic you are essentially poisoning yourself. Instead, it might be worthwhile to realise that keeping company with negative vampires is like walking in the mist and expecting your clothes to stay dry. No matter what you do, you will be affected – one way or the other.

Have you ever found yourself saying, "I am sick and tired of being in this relationship with you?" Or do others repeatedly hear you saying: "I am sick and tired of this whole situation. It's driving me crazy." This linguistic cue is evidence that you unconsciously know the cause of your 'undiagnosable' illnesses. Your relationship is draining you of energy; tapping into your source and using it without giving anything back to you. You are the 'filling station' for these illnesses, yet you cannot work out why you feel such resentment. Take an objective look at the people with whom you choose to spend your valuable time and consider deleting those who you know take you for granted. Instead, choose to share yourself with those who magnify your potential, who open your eyes to possibilities – do not keep investing in people who always leave you feeling hopeless.

Our relationships should be mutual and healthy. We owe that to each other and to ourselves. If you keep telling yourself that you are not getting enough rest and are suffering some sort of physical and mental breakdown, consider making some changes to remedy the situation. Possibly you are literally sick because your body is drained and your mind is working overtime. Pay closer attention to both the messages you send to yourself and to the messages you receive.

If you are sharing space or spending time with someone who chronically discusses their ailments with you, ask them if this is the best way they have of attracting your attention. People do learn to use their pain for gain.

Make a commitment to yourself to really *hear* the language of your body because as your body heals, so will your mind, and as your mind heals, so will your body.

Sleeping styles

Sleep is possibly the most underestimated part of our day. Bad sleep results in poor performance, deteriorating health and mood swings. Good rest is essential if we want to regenerate and refresh our bodies and minds. It is the key to physical and mental health, and it slows down the ageing process and reduces stress.

If you inherited a low stress threshold or have a history of mental disorders (genetic or otherwise), lack of sleep can trigger those pathologies. It is therefore very important to manage your stress levels and create a quiet sleeping place – especially if you are vulnerable to personality changes when you are tired. It also helps a great deal to have a routine, to wake and sleep at similar times each day.

Do you or your partner continually fall asleep in front of the TV? Do you consume too much alcohol? Alcohol is a depressant as well as a sleep disturber. So once the cycle starts, it picks up in pace – if you drink to fall asleep you are likely to be restless at night and will feel tired the next day, which in turn causes stress and then results in more drinking.

If one person is an anxious type and has to get up at 2am because they are restless, the sleep of the other will be disturbed. Both partners then end up being stressed because one keeps the other awake. Generally, the main reasons for waking up in the middle of the night are guilt and shame and unresolved issues; things left unsaid and undone. These are at the root of worry.

How do you feel about being woken up when you are fast asleep? Are you possessive about your escapism time? How peacefully did you sleep as a child? If you were in an environment of abuse or parental fighting or loud noises that made you feel unsafe, you will need a very quiet sleeping space so that you can totally relax and let go. Otherwise, you will be constantly monitoring noises.

Do your sleep patterns match those of your partner? Are you an owl and she a lark? Also look at age and personality differences. Does he get too hot and you get too cold? Snoring can seriously affect and destroy an essentially good relationship. Look for solutions because sleep deprivation can adversely affect everything in your life. It is not for nothing that some military forces use sleep deprivation as a means of torturing their enemies.

Some people say they prefer living apart from their relationship partner because then at least they get a chance to catch up on sleep and rejuvenate themselves! If living apart is not an option, are separate bedrooms the answer? There seems to be a trend towards this, although most people do not speak about it openly. The downside of this option is that it does create distance. People drift away from one another and at least one of the partners will resent it. It is important to maintain intimacy within a committed relationship otherwise the cracks between you become very wide, wide enough for someone else to step into. Finding a way to create a shared sleeping space and dreamtime is important in terms of intimacy in a relationship.

BEING EMOTIONALLY HEALTHY

✥

I bring to you the message of balance… be in harmony with yourself and those around you, and all will be well.

✥

Stuffing versus starving

Changing our body shape by gaining or losing weight can be used as a means of achieving stability within our relationships as well as a means of finding a new one. Not all relationships are centred on physical appearance, but subtle indoctrination by society can trick us into thinking that we are not worthy of a relationship unless we conform to what someone else has decided is the perfect form. And when we are feeling vulnerable and unworthy, we will default to what we see and hear via the media as being desirable and potentially 'happiness-creating.'

The decision to follow what we see and hear in our external worlds is not always a conscious choice. We sometimes blindly follow others – and the media. If you decide that you want to change your physical self to be perfect for another, you should ask yourself whether this is a kind way to treat yourself. Are people really more attentive when you have a different body shape? Or was it perhaps the fact that you had a better relationship with yourself and you felt healthier and therefore were happier when relating to others? Were there perhaps other issues at that happy time – unrelated to your looks – that you now believe were entirely due to you looking as you did then?

Boundaries and victims

Gaining weight is also one of the more subtle ways in which we create protective boundaries around our emotions. When we feel vulnerable and unsafe, we choose different ways of shielding ourselves from others. Fat forms a comforting buffer against the sharpness of the outside world. It is a big 'fear cushion.' But why do we feel that we need to protect ourselves physically when the threat is an emotional one? When we are exposed to real danger, our body goes into fight-or-flight mode. This is our body's instinctive response to a real threat, albeit only a perceived one, and we prepare to take action to protect ourselves and sometimes to protect others.

In situations of emotional fear, the threat is internal and not necessarily external. We feel fearful of being hurt inside. In these circumstances, we are in a double bind – we innately desire love and affection, but fear it too; therefore, we decide to compromise. "I will not take flight, I will stay here in my body but will not let anyone get close to me. I will start building barriers up from the inside." In that way we protect ourselves from hurt and so minimise our fear. In this way we think we can shield our psychological and emotional selves from pain. It is very important for us to know that we have the right to express our vulnerability as much as we have the right to enjoy being nurtured.

If – over the years – you learned to anaesthetise your sensitivity to the world through eating, it becomes your habit and your way of feeling organised and in control. You may have become accustomed to people referring to you as self-sufficient and independent and reliable. You serve the needs of others at your expense and you do not want others to know your sensitive side.

Having no boundaries means you are incapable of saying 'no' to taking responsibility for the emotions and needs of others. Because we have been trained to serve others and to be 'nice', being 'not-nice' equals the very real possibility of rejection. As a solution, we put a barrier around ourselves that we hope will cushion the blow from the harshness of others. And when we feel disarmed and disempowered, we eat more to pad out our armour. If we feel we are not getting the emotional support we need from others when we feel fragile, we resort to self-comfort through eating. It is a false sense of security; a way of pacifying our fear of having our hurt feelings revealed to others – protection by means of tasty self-sabotage.

"Why do people never appreciate what I do…if I were thin they would…the world isn't fair." But maybe you fear intimacy and you are unconsciously creating a body that you think no-one will want to caress? Does the wall of weight perhaps make you feel safe? And is it easier to blame your weight for the 'injustice' you feel, than to look at the real reasons why you're trying to keep people away?

Our fear cushion can also form part of how we justify our singleness or any other circumstance in our lives where we feel a sense of being rejected by others. We make fat the excuse and the reason for these feelings: "He doesn't like me because I'm fat" is less threatening than the implied, "He doesn't like me because I'm me."

Sometimes we sabotage ourselves to make others feel better about themselves because we feel guilty for being born with a 'normal' body. If someone in your immediate environment (a sibling or another close family member, perhaps) has a physical deformity or disability, you may attempt to 'deform' or 'diminish' yourself by negatively altering your body shape to pacify their insecurities. To fit in and to belong. You may be constantly reminded of how lucky you are to be 'perfect' and could start taking this on as a disadvantage because it feels as if this is being held against you. Therefore, if you too developed a physical deformity, you would be more accepted and be part of the norm. This is usually an unconscious decision, coupled with other behaviour, which is often motivated by feelings of guilt because you are not suffering or in physical pain.

We normally focus on women with eating disorders, but men also experience this problem. One of the root causes of eating disorders in men can be traced back to teasing and bullying at school. They might have been the target of hurtful jokes and feel rejected; they do not fit in. In response, some could start working out to be stronger and thinner or take up martial arts. "One day I'll get you back", they decide. Others may find a loyal friend in food.

It is important to note that the underlying psychological factors leading to an eating disorder are the same for both men and women. These are depression, a low self-esteem and the need to be accepted. Generally these individuals do not cope well with their emotions and personal issues.

Gay men may go through a period of internal struggle with expressing their sexuality and feel particularly unable to do so in the workplace and with family. This emotional stress can also result in eating disorders. Male body image has become increasingly important in the gay community, and this places a high expectation on physical appearance. Everyone wants to present with the perceived 'ideal body image', especially when chatting up that cute boy. Unfortunately, an unhealthy preoccupation with our bodies can lead to physical insecurities and sometimes even steroid use.

On the other hand, two women in a gay relationship may put on piles of weight to cushion themselves against being tempted to cheat or to signal that they are settled and not available.

There is no judgment about how you choose to be in your body. If you feel you have found the right fit, then that fit is the perfect one for you. However, you need to look at the attitude you have towards yourself. How do you feel about who you are? Remember that what you give out others will reflect back to you. We really do need to pay attention when we are damaging ourselves.

If your shape is not comfortable for you, you have the choice to open the door. No-one can get through your walls unless you invite them in. Begin by taking small chances with your emotions. Maybe start by displaying little treats of yourself to those around you. Be open and you will be surprised at how much support you will receive – often from the most unexpected sources.

Can you ever be too thin?

How is it that we learn to enjoy excessive weight loss? Why does this unhealthy skinniness work for you and do you really feel more accepted? Are you truly being acknowledged for all that you are and is this recognition coming from the right type of person? But what is the right type of person? Usually this is someone with whom you can share what is important to you and in whose company you can like yourself as who you truly are.

If you want to use this 'thin technique' to gain recognition, you will get the kind of relationship that this draws. If you start dating someone who says he really likes you because you look so good in a tiny pair of jeans, do not be surprised when – six months down the line – you find yourself saying, "I don't know what more I can do, he is always looking at other thin women. I never feel good enough." Is this person having a relationship with you or with a skinny woman?

Sometimes being little and fragile is useful if you need a guardian. You may be someone who needs to be looked after in a relationship because you do not want to carry the weight of having adult responsibilities. Or perhaps there was a lack of affection and attention by a significant parent when you were growing up and you are still trying to recapture and rectify that lost relationship by staying in a child-like body. Being unhealthily thin means you are damaging yourself for a pay-off. You need to take an honest look at your situation and decide – is this really worth it for me?

Pregnancy

Some marriages are designed around traditional roles. In these circumstances the expectation is that the woman will perpetuate the family line. If she does not, she might be viewed as an incomplete woman; someone not performing her duty to womankind. However, as soon as she does become pregnant, she is showered with attention and adoration. She puts on weight and feels happy and voluptuous and feminine – and her partner and others are admiring her belly and stroking her unborn child. Her current body shape works well for her now because she feels totally validated and accepted. But, in later *unpregnant* years, the situation does not feel the same and she may have a need to recapture the special feeling she experienced when pregnant, because she cherishes the memory of how that circumstance rewarded her in the past.

During her pregnancy, she became conditioned and she programmed herself into thinking that her worthiness – in others' eyes – was dependant on her looking fertile and pregnant. If she loses weight now, she will not look fertile anymore and she thinks that this will cause her to lose her attractiveness and usefulness to her husband. Her being in this relationship has become conditional. Albeit unconscious, she will put on weight in order to salvage her position, and because of her positive past programming she will feel that this could place her in a favourable light – of being viewed as 'possibly pregnant' – and she will therefore receive the desired attention and feel useful again. The sad reality is that her husband is more likely to perceive her as being fat and out of control, and on some level she must be aware of that. "Why can't I lose the weight that I put it on when I was pregnant?"

Do you really want to lose it or is it serving some purpose for you?

Telling the truth

As the images form in your mind and trickle down into your mouth, do you end up swallowing your words? This behaviour of word block-ing often develops when previous attempts at self-expression have resulted in punishment or your opinion has been left unrecognized and unacknowledged. If you have a need to have your emotions validated by a specific person or people, you will want to say the right things – the things that you think they want to hear.

We may want others to affirm our worthiness and we will do anything necessary to maintain our position in the relationship; but we do not feel safe enough to allow the true vulnerability of our feelings to shine through. We cannot speak our truth because we believe it will cause us to be rejected by others. So we try to manage ourselves in ways that we think are more appropriate – ways that are easier to stomach.

"I just don't say anything anymore. It's easier that way," you tell your friends.

But is it? And easier on whom? This self-imposed silence is a short-term strategy; and an attempt at salvaging self worth.

In the past, people may have said, "Don't listen to her, she knows nothing". Or, "He doesn't know what he's talking about". You will eventually learn – through these experiences – to believe that your opinion holds no value and that nothing you say changes anything. In fact, when you have voiced an idea or a feeling, the outcome has left you feeling less validated and more rejected.

Maybe when you did express yourself, it caused disharmony and you were unfairly blamed for unrelated issues. So you decided to keep quiet rather than cause a bad vibe. But, over time, saying nothing becomes the bad vibe and you end up avoiding going home to your partner and you find yourself spending more time out with your friends than with your partner in an effort to keep the peace.

As a child, were you trained to gain acceptance by being seen and not heard? But, where does that leave you now as an adult? All those unspoken words have built up and clogged your throat over the years – and you wonder why you suffer from a chronic sore throat and neck pain or maybe even thyroid problems. Maybe it is the person you refer to as a 'pain in the neck' who is the one you keep quiet for? Sometimes you do this to keep your job; sometimes to pacify a partner or a family member; or sometimes simply for fear of disturbing a comfortable situation; or maybe you stay silent because of an unresolved fear of change.

Somewhere in our early life we may have learned that laying bare our emotions causes pain because we did not receive the appropriate reinforcement or response we needed at the time. Our emotions were not nurtured, pacified and supported and our expressions were not valued, appreciated or recognised. So, in order not to recreate that pain, we've taken a decision to arm ourselves with silence. We've decided to be strong by being silent.

But, in so doing, we actually make ourselves weak because the amount of energy it takes to maintain unhealthy boundaries – to keep on fighting – makes us tired and we cannot understand why we're tired all the time. Ultimately, we dissociate ourselves from ourselves. We inhibit having a loving relationship with ourselves because by building walls against others, we also build them against knowing who we are. Later on in life, we may start asking: "Who am I?" and "Why do I feel so unfulfilled?"

Learn to speak your truth – it is not only what you say, but how you say it, that is important. Speak with kindness and all will be well with you.

Time-related emotional needs

It can be useful to look at your history and explore the origins of your need to use your physical form to attain feelings of worthiness. Was there a time when your physical form changed during a specific emotional incident?

As we grow physically and the shape of our body changes, we are simultaneously going through different life experiences. How we are in our bodies and how we are living and expressing our emotions at different times become intertwined and interconnected. In this way, our looks, our image, and our experiences at important times in our lives are intertwined, and our minds associate one with the other.

When you were a young boy, how did it make you feel to see your shoulders broaden and your height increasing? Were you ready to step into manhood, or were you feeling diminished as your voice broke? Or as a girl entering womanhood, did you appreciate the swelling of your breasts, the widening of your hips and the disappearance of your puppy fat? What was happening in your immediate environment during these important milestone events? Did you have enough support and nurturing during your metamorphosis or were you left to find your own wings?

Think of incidences in your past that were happening at the time that you were experiencing major changes in your physical body, and consider how they could have left you feeling unsafe and fragile.

Was there a loss of someone close to you? Did you move away from a familiar environment? Did you feel unaccepted by your peers? Was there a threat of rejection from someone in whom you had invested your emotional energy? Did you start receiving inappropriate sexual advances from people you trusted? Or was there a threat that you then perceived and processed to be one of life and death? The way your body was feeling then will be remembered by your mind and coupled with the prevailing emotional experience.

Sometimes neutral information can be incorrectly processed, such as when a child becomes too old to cuddle up in bed with his or her parents and is told that this nurturing is no longer appropriate. Suddenly that child has to deal with touch deprivation and remembers it as a consequence of growing up.

Ideally, any move from one developmental stage into the next should be an exciting experience. It could be celebrated as a milestone event and the child could be affirmed and rewarded for going into something new instead of being pushed away from something familiar.

When we are in a space of fear, the drive is to overcome our fear as quickly as possible – and we will do so by choosing the easiest and most familiar route known to us at the time. So, if gaining acceptance and numbing the pain of rejection mean turning on ourselves, we will take this particular path. If this behaviour is positively reinforced, and the people around us start giving us encouraging feedback, we will feel that we have achieved our goal. The primary thought we will store is: "In this form I am acceptable and therefore safe." Or, "I am a fat, happy, caring person. If I lose weight, no-one will like me because they know me like this. If I change, I will be rejected." Alternatively, "I am skinny and fragile and if I put on weight I will have to look after myself."

When we are feeling unfulfilled, our thoughts regress to times when we think we were happier than we are now; times when the pay-off for our behaviour was greatest; times when we felt accepted.

Look at how your posture has changed over the years. Did you keep one 'shape' just to attract someone and then discard this way of being later on in life? Why? Have your shoulders become more rounded because you are carrying too big a burden? Have you developed lower back pain as financial fears crept in? Can you still stand on your own two feet or have circumstances left you feeling as if you are on shaky ground? Do you feel that the rug is constantly being pulled out from under you?

You may find that you become unhappy with yourself when you are feeling unhealthy. When you are unhappy, you will tend to self sabotage. It becomes easier to smoke more, or to have one more drink, or to eat that extra slab of delicious chocolate because you tell yourself, "I feel bad anyhow, so what's the difference; I may as well go the whole way and totally toxin myself out." This is how an unhealthy cycle of self sabotage starts – and only you can break it.

Consider whether you are doing unhealthy things to yourself because your relationship with yourself is unhappy and unfulfilled. Consider which shape is really best for you – discover the shape that honestly represents your truth. And do what it takes to become that.

Body decorations

If we do not change our actual physical body shape to draw attention, we may change how we decorate it. We think back to all those happy times when life was 'perfect' and we want to play that role again, so we dress up to act the part. This might be a vain attempt at regaining feelings of happiness when everything else around us has changed and we look different too.

Generally, if we see someone wearing overly tight or revealing clothing, or if we encounter someone who dyes their hair bright orange, they are usually someone who is looking for some sort of attention. They do not feel worthy being 'just me'. Sometimes, however, we can go through phases of redefining ourselves in which we really need to separate from our old identity. We want our inner changes to be tangible and externally obvious to others and to ourselves. It may be that you would like to be more independent from your partner, but cannot move away, so you give subtle clues to hint at your new personality. You think, "I will change my hair colour and my hair style" or "I will wear these revealing clothes." Men may put on weight and grow a beard in order to separate their old identity from their new one; to be taken more seriously perhaps? Sometimes we need to assume a new role to get recognition, to stand out, and we broadcast a different image of ourselves through our revised external presentation.

Other ways of changing our external look can include having our skin tattooed or pierced. But, why is it that if you do choose to market yourself in this way that you become so upset when someone buys into your campaign and stereotypes you? They only want what the package says, not the original product. Unfortunately, the society in which we live frames us according to our appearance. Others decide – based on our body representation – what and who we are. If you see someone walking down the street in a white coat with a stethoscope hanging around their neck, your instinctive thought will be "this is a doctor". In the same way, we tend to categorise others according to their dress code. This is just the way it is in the world. You need to be objective about how you project yourself to others, and try to see yourself realistically.

Ultimately, you will get what you ask for – so expect a response. If you tell the world, "my worthiness is dependent on your response to my physical presentation," the Universe will respond by sending you people who pacify that need. You will draw in those who are interested only in your created image – your branded clothing and your expensive sunglasses. When you hear yourself saying, "Everyone I know is so shallow and materialistic," ask yourself, "Why am I attracting these people? Why am I sending the messages that I'm sending, and for whom? What am I hiding behind?"

We should always remember that our bodies are the vehicle for our souls. They provide the means whereby we can act out our physical journey on this planet. Be sure to ask yourself, "Does he or she love me for who I am – or do they want me for what I can do for them and how I make them feel?"

Asking for help

It is very useful to accept help from others and to recognise that you cannot do everything for yourself, by yourself. From time to time, you will need energy from an outside source to help you to get back on track. Sometimes we become like spinning tops and we lose sight of the fact that we are out of balance. It is very useful to find someone whom you trust to help you find your centre again. Whether you choose body stress release therapy, kinesiology, reiki or massage – or any other way of finding your balance again – make sure that you choose someone with the right energy, someone who feels like the right person to be helping you.

Listen to yourself and take note of what is happening to you. Having a healthy body means that you will have a healthy mind, and a healthy mind in turn creates a healthy body. You owe it to yourself to pay attention to your body … it is the temple of your soul.

Sabotaging the self

We can define sabotage as any act that causes deliberate damage to some-one or something so that they become unable to function. Arenas that are vulnerable to sabotage are wars, the workplace, valuable resources and our interpersonal relationships. When waging a war, sabotage is targeted at destroying the infrastructure that sustains a country in order to gain territorial advantage. Workplace sabotage typically occurs in environments in which there is discontentment amongst members of staff. They want their demands met and – until such time – they will continue to hamper production or destroy equipment. Crimes of sabotage targeted at valuable resources usually involve individuals who extort large sums of money from companies by threatening to destroy something of value belonging to the company if they are not compensated. In essence, sabotage is a deliberate act of destruction or disruption for a specific pay-off and most of us would – more than likely – not support the pay-off someone has in mind.

However, whether or not we are conscious of our actions, many of us sabotage our interpersonal relationships. Have you ever found yourself deciding to go on a diet, stop drinking, or give up smoking and then noticed how your decision affects others? For example, if you were to attend a social function with your friends, you may find that your evening is punctuated with comments such as, "I made this pudding especially for you – just have a small piece?" or "Don't tell me you don't want a drink? What's your problem?" Why is it that another's decision to treat himself or herself with more respect is sabotaged?

There are various reasons that we tend to sabotage our own decisions or the decisions of others, but whatever the reason there will be a pay-off involved. Even if there appears to be a genuine lack of understanding about a particular choice, the saboteur still feels the need to assert their will over yours by assuming that you are depriving yourself of something that always used to make you feel good. This is usually something they did for you that made them feel worthy. Most often in sabotage situations, a root of insecurity is being tugged.

If you decide to change your behaviour, this sometimes translates into others feeling insecure because to them you are no longer controllable or predictable. This 'new you' can also bring out a competitive streak in those around you and if you could hear their thoughts, they may sound something like this, "He has stopped drinking and smoking and looks really healthy and fit. What can I do to diminish that? He needs to come down a peg or two." Are we really more comfortable reducing everyone to the lowest common denominator?

You may recognise different forms of sabotage playing out in committed relationships. Have you ever found yourself feeling threatened by your partner's success or popularity? Maybe in these instances you would choose to fight back by chipping away at your partner's self-esteem in an attempt to maintain your own, and keep them in their place – their place being somewhere where you feel that they are under your control.

"Have you seen Harold lately? He is doing so well – he just bought a yacht and a new apartment. Maybe one day you'll get there."

However, sometimes sabotaging a relationship can be due to a phobia about commitment. Either there is a real fear of commitment; or you are with someone to whom you do not wish to commit, but you don't have the courage to leave yet. So, instead of ending the relationship, you continually puncture it because you neither want it, nor do you want to leave.

When we choose to sabotage ourselves, we slip into a form of victim mentality. We will set about creating situations to prove that life is difficult; that we have bad luck. "Life is not meant to be easy," you may tell yourself as you set about creating your personal drama. When things go too well you may disrupt the flow and create chaos. Possibly you fear happiness or perhaps the thought of achieving your goals scares you – because *then what*?

We may also end up sabotaging ourselves, through our behaviour, into loneliness and isolation. In this case, the melodrama addict holds a sympathetic person hostage; they become the victim's victim. In other cases people can be hooked on telling their stories over and over, canvassing advice they never take because they are terrified of the vacuum that might result from dropping their story.

Do you know anyone who insists on filling silences with unending vacuous chatter so no one can get a personal question in edgewise? Or the friend who is always busy, on the way out, doing altruistic deeds but emotionally unavailable to those who hope to love them? There are also good listeners who observe others, never themselves; who usually have a few new age quotes up their sleeves to divert attention. These behaviours can be seen as a subtle form of self-sabotage because they succeed in creating a circumstance of isolation; basically through the person's lack of awareness of self and of others. Or because they do not want others to know that they can be affected by their emotions.

Apart from hampering our life-situations, we may also resort to self sabotage as a distorted means of dealing with or processing a sensation. At best, our self sabotage is an attempt to focus and make tangible feelings that can neither be defined nor placed. The degree to which you feel you do not deserve to live is directly proportional to your desire for self sabotage. In other words, if you perceive that you do not have the right to be alive, you will continually engage in self-sabotaging behaviour.

Such feelings of worthlessness might lead you to engage in impulsive and self-damaging behaviour such as indiscriminate sex, abuse of substances or reckless driving.

Those who lacked adequate role models in childhood may not understand and integrate healthy ways of expressing a range of emotions (from fear through to love) and will most likely not know how to express healthy feelings of worthiness. They can learn – through conditioning – to identify pain as a means of experiencing a feeling. By identifying corporal punishment as a form of attention or acknowledgment, no punishment could feel like rejection. Not all feelings are converted into pain, but pain becomes the means through which the concept of feeling is understood. Ultimately a link between love and pain is formed – love equals pain and pain equals love. For self-saboteurs this becomes the known, comfortable, and familiar way of relating to themselves and others.

If feelings – other than pain – enter our realm, they will be perceived as foreign and threatening, and our primary response will be to set up defenses against these emotions. They will need to be dulled and numbed because there is no known means of dealing with them. When one's guarded arena of safety is under threat, the default route will be to anaesthetise oneself and exist unconsciously.

One of the more socially acceptable forms of self-sabotage is using others as your tool. Instead of physically cutting yourself, you will find someone to slice you up emotionally.

"I will allow someone else to sabotage me so that I don't have to do it to myself; or because I don't get the right feeling when I do it to myself."

The 'right' feeling sometimes involves satisfying an underlying need for punishment. You do not feel that you deserve respectful attention because you find yourself sinful and worthless. There could possibly be guilt transferred from your parents; maybe your mother felt ashamed or was kept hidden when she was pregnant with you? Her feelings became your fault.

In these circumstances, you will choose someone who – like yourself – does not understand healthy emotional interaction. Your choice of person could be narcissistic or ego-driven in nature and detached from feeling the slightest touch of selfless emotion. These people often have a misguided idea of who they really are, as they have spent much of their lives creating an 'ideal self', a masked self to be the person they think others will admire. Their inferiority complex is replaced by a superiority complex and they tend to devalue others in their quest for excessive admiration. Possibly, at some time in the narcissist's emotional journey, they may have been spoilt and given unrealistic 'limelight' attention by a parent, causing them to develop an inflated view of themselves. Ironically, they are often jealous of those who feel good about themselves and are typically drawn to those with a low self-esteem because of their own egocentric nature. These people need to be revered. Their mantra could be, "You owe me, but I will give you nothing."

In other circumstances an individual may have learned that expressing their emotions was too risky. They could have been closely bonded to someone – this may have been a parent who died when they were at a vulnerable age, or a girlfriend or a boyfriend who cracked their heart at a fragile point. They felt betrayed when they allowed themselves to expose their emotions because the reward was emptiness and loss. "I will shut down my feelings now because it's not worth it. I choose to feel nothing."

The similarity between the saboteur and the sabotaged is that they both have had their emotional wiring crossed and have learned to relate in fear rather than in love. Whether it was due to permissive or punitive parenting, or an experience of rejection or betrayal by another, they learned that normal interrelating within a relationship means that there has to be adrenalin, an acute intensity. Without this intensity there is no real relationship for them, because real relationships are spiced with tension and cannot be dull and boring.

The saboteur acts out his or her issues and feels validated in the knowledge that these actions are creating an emotional response in the other. They see their emotions enacted and represented externally in the behaviour of their partner. Their internal turmoil happens somewhere out there in the objective realm. They flick a switch and the other behaves. The sabotaged one becomes an expression of their inability to understand and hold their own feelings within themselves. The saboteur looks on and becomes the voyeur to their own emotional confusion and feels safety in the fact that the sabotaged party never leaves them – no matter what they do. And it is interesting to note that it is usually women who allow themselves to be bullied and belittled by men. This – realistically – cannot be the only type of relationship in which this sabotage occurs, but it is the one that we encounter most often.

The question that we need to consider is this: Why would someone want to stay in a hostile environment with another who has a need to be punitive? The answer is generally quite simple: because they are in a comfort zone. The sabotaged one feels bonded and affirmed and 'visible' because he or she is in pain. And if that feeling is aroused, it must be right; they feel loved. Physical abuse perpetuates in a relationship because the relationship is built on misguided ideas of what true feelings are.

She will say, "He hits me because he loves me," or "He is so jealous of me – it means he loves me. And he doesn't even want me to go out by myself, he cares that much."

People who abuse others are generally saturated with feelings of anger and resentment, and they most often carry complexes of inferiority and insecurity. Anyone who has the need to violate another generally cannot sustain a loving relationship with themselves.

Familiar zones

But where did we learn to feel comfortable in an environment that is so blatantly uncomfortable? When did the safe, familiar comfort zone become associated with pain? Being addicted to something can offer one of two pay-offs: it either stills the emotional pain, or it gives us a feeling – not as it should be – but a feeling nonetheless. At least we can sense something. Maybe, as a child, the only time you were ever touched by your primary caregiver was when you were given a hiding or smacked. For you then, pain equals love. Especially when you are told: "I'm hitting you because I love you." Or "You are being punished because I care about you."

Our pattern becomes one of being addicted to finding someone who will put a toxic needle into our arm to anaesthetise us so that we cannot find ourselves. And we will go back for more because it becomes a fix; a zone of 'normality'.

However, an abuser cannot act out abuse on another without causing damage to him or herself. But the abused gives the abuser permission, because this way of being makes the abused feel accepted and special. If, as a child, you gained acceptance and acknowledgement when you were beaten, it was how you received your touch attention. You were trained to take the blame for something that was not your fault by being ordered to go and apologise to the person who beat you. So, later on in life you choose someone to be your poison and you ingest that poison every day. And you keep saying, "I'm sorry. It's my fault. I'll try harder."

Reality checks

How could you possibly believe that someone loves you when they are abusing you? Maybe you live in fear and cannot express your self worth because you are not giving yourself the opportunity to find your self. Maybe this is your reality – you identify with it because you are already damaged. And your reality says, "*This is love*", and you believe it. This is how your life will continue until you find another way of expressing your self worth.

If you do not respect yourself, no-one else will show you respect either. The people you engage with will continually reinforce your negative self-image because that is what makes them feel good. Broken people hook into each other's darkest issues to feel fixed in some way. You are both engaging in a relationship in the best way that you know how, because neither of you has developed a loving relationship with self; you have no true self-love. If you did, you would be whole enough not to be attracted to those whose only desire is to break you. However, you are responding to inefficient programming and are reinforcing the habit by staying together. Nothing changes and you will remain stuck in the vortex of abuse for as long as you choose to spin there.

Boredom

If you are feeling bored in your relationship, you are most likely not doing things that bring you joy. You might be waiting for your partner to entertain you and validate you. Sometimes we overcompensate and focus our attention on pacifying the other's insecurities, and in so doing we neglect our interests and our own lives. A relationship is not meant to sustain us and give us our will to live. We cannot give another the responsibility of maintaining our self-worth. If your emotions are intertwined with the behaviour of your partner and you feel stuck and anaesthetized, this indicates that you are co-dependent. You should ask yourself, "Am I living my life, or am I just waiting to see what they do first?"

Insecurities

You need to learn to deal with insecurities in whichever way works for you. Do not allow yourself to be disabled by living with mistrust and inferiority issues. If you are in a relationship where you are being made to feel inferior, look at your interactions more objectively. Are they deliberately making you feel insecure to pacify their own needs? Or are you perhaps projecting your past experience unfairly onto your current partner?

Frustration

Frustration is anger repressed. When the anger we feel towards someone or a situation goes unexpressed, we start to hint. We become a pressure-cooker, letting off intense spurts of steam, but never venting anything fully. All the heat boils, bubbles, and stays trapped inside. Why are you angry in the first place? Are you perhaps angry with yourself for allowing your self-worth to be compromised?

Happiness

"I can make you happy" is a promise that can't come true. You are responsible for finding an environment that fulfills you. No-one can make you happy except yourself.

Addictions

If we cannot find someone else to give us a 'feeling', what do we do? How else do we actively run away from ourselves in our ongoing attempts at avoiding reality?

We turn to addictions. An addiction becomes our primary relationship. The addiction becomes 'the special one' on whom we rely to provide us with a (false) sense of security. These are the friendly, familiar and ever-present false allies whom we believe will provide us with the feeling that we interpret as love – a euphoric, anaesthetized delusion. We therefore create a void by doing something vacuous, and then we fill it with what created it in the first place. In other words, we lay down unstable emotional foundations by neglecting ourselves and we avoid engaging in a caring relationship with ourselves. Eventually, we will lose sight of who we are and we become more reliant on others to define us.

So you end up having an empty life and you wonder why you feel depressed. Life experiences become totally dependent on staying anesthetised and you become more dependent on – and more desperate for – external stimulation and input because you are full of 'nothing' and therefore generate nothing.

For the purposes of this book, we will define the words *addict* and *addiction* to represent those people and situations in which a relationship with a drug of choice is prioritised over honest relationships with self and other people. There has to be an obvious dependence on the drug of choice and the addict's day must be structured around their habit; they surrender their personal power to their addiction. They insert a toxin into their minds – or into their bodies – and they become enslaved.

It is sad but true that our emotional development gets stuck the moment we hand our personalities over to an addictive lifestyle. Why? Because the substance or choice of addiction remains the same regardless of our emotions. Our addiction does not challenge us or encourage us to engage in new ways of behaving in its relationship with us. The addiction is unresponsive in itself, yet it causes a response within us. The addiction stays as it is and we stay as we are; and we welcome the predictability of its non-judgment. Some people turn to substance abuse in an attempt to deal with an emotional crisis; they turn to drink or become homeless because of job loss or the death of a spouse later on in life. Others try to avoid emotional experiences and take to drugs in their teenage years – as adults they then continue to relate to life as emotional adolescents. But is this really rewarding; can we honestly enjoy ourselves like this?

Addictive behaviour resembles obsessive compulsive disorder (OCD) in the way that an addict's mindset has constant intrusive thoughts about his or her addiction of choice. They are trapped in a circumstance of anxiety that holds them, creates them, and maintains them. Their thoughts are consumed with acting out what they need to do in order to calm the restless chatter. And the little voice keeps calling out from the bottom of the slippery slope, "Come to my altar and worship me."

Research has shown that people who start using nicotine as teenagers have a very high possibility of developing some form of anxiety disorder as an adult. What fears were you experiencing in your adolescent years that you learned to pacify through nicotine abuse? Tobacco in itself causes physical sensations of anxiety, so each time you light up in later years, you will unconsciously remind yourself of those early, unsafe days and then have another cigarette to help erase that unpleasant memory. Nicotine reminds you of why you started smoking in the first place, and keeps the reason alive in your psyche. It is a conditioned response. Like a pigeon with a lever; you keep pressing, but you've forgotten why.

As your relationship with tobacco becomes a bit stale, you may want to introduce more substances into the mix to have more experiences and to encourage different types of feelings. You want an exciting outing with new opportunities. Ironically, you are going nowhere because with addictions you are stuck in the mud with the handbrake on. Your relationship with yourself will be put on hold because your primary relationship is with your drug of choice.

Life choices

But why would anyone choose to stay trapped within this unhealthy lifestyle? Maybe you are too scared to experience your emotions because they are unfamiliar sensations. Maybe you assume that being unfeeling is a strength and that having feelings creates weakness – so therefore *not* feeling becomes your protection. When you started gambling or using alcohol or other substances, you might have been looking for something to block your heart – to pacify your vulnerability – because you were never nurtured properly and do not understand what it means to feel emotionally safe. So, in desperation you turned to something to pacify the inconsistencies and the insecurities of an unpredictable environment, something to even out the bumps. And now you turn to addictive behaviour to feel normal because without this ritual you feel lost. Maybe your early environment had too many rules and no heart. Maybe acceptance was conditional? "I would love you if…" And now you say you have a poker face – no-one will ever know what you're thinking or feeling behind the mask; you've become so good at hiding.

If the primary focus is not to feel, how do you protect yourself from intrusive feelings of softness? Maybe you adrenalise yourself by forming a pseudo-barrier against intrusive feelings. Maybe check that your drug of choice really satisfies the position of a primary relationship. Ask yourself how many human relationships you have sacrificed in order to prioritise your addiction. We are sociable beings and are meant to have relationships with other people. Substances do not care. They are neutral until we give them life and status in our lives.

Emotional escape

How far are you willing to run to escape from yourself and your emotions – and for how long? Because the period of escapism will eventually end; you will burn out, longing for love.

If you were never properly taught how to relate in a healthy way in a relationship, the chances are that you will have no idea what a mutually loving and supportive relationship is. So, how can you recognise it when you see it?

You might be more inclined to settle for something that you think you understand and that you think you can control – something you perceive as reliable and consistent and always there for you. But is it there for your highest good? Do you really feel nurtured and loved and appreciated?

Perhaps you haven't chosen drugs, or alcohol, or gambling as your primary relationship choice – you might have chosen adrenalin as the easiest way to rid yourself of a feeling or several intrusive feelings. You successfully override any possible emotional pain by detaching from yourself; by observing your heart rate and your breathing instead of your feelings. The obvious route to choose then would be to have a workout. To sweat it out with excessive exercise. Anytime anyone gets too close, you will have to numb your emotions with an endorphin rush, and sometimes even with physical pain.

Maybe you choose to start another course of study to ensure that all your thoughts and potential emotions are tied up in cerebral analysis. In that way your feelings become academic theories and you do not have to sit with the insecurity of dealing with any foreign and uncomfortable emotions. "I think therefore I don't have to feel…"

What about the empty expectation of an addiction to sex? A typical example is the classic serial monogamist who has to 'try out' many different people to get the same rush, because one person may just get too close for comfort. It must be remembered that sexual encounters are not necessarily intimate and people often use random sexual encounters to avoid intimacy. A circumstance of meeting someone online or via e-mail cannot be seen as growing intimacy. It is most likely a high that comes from being addicted to the infatuation. Then once reality sets in and the person becomes real and available, the compulsion is over; the obsession is pacified. The goal has been achieved and the drug becomes stagnant, boring and too passive, so the acting has to stop and you have to be real – which means you have to find a new obsession. In these circumstances you may want to ask yourself, "Do I know who I am?" Maybe you fear that your fragmented personality could be exposed if you stay still in the company of one person for too long, and that you could lose control of your mask juggling act.

Gambling is considered to be more of an impulse control disorder than an obsessive compulsive disorder (OCD). Gambling is – especially in men – often rooted in the absence of a father when the child was under the age of seven. This parent may have died or have been absent shortly after birth. Believing that one has the magical ability to control numbers and money becomes the game and it creates the adrenalin needed to numb the emotional pain. Staying in your head and out of your heart gives back some of the control that you felt you lost in the chaos of your childhood; the chaos in which you felt unable to pacify and solve your mother's emotional problems. The wires got crossed. Hope became entwined with fear.

"I hope I'll be safe, but I fear I'm not. I hope I win at the casino tonight, but I fear I may lose."

Addictions are all forms of anxiety, and anxiety is born of fear. You act out addictive behaviour if your self-worth is not intact. It is directly related to the integrity of your relationship with yourself and how worthy you feel in the environment in which you engage. Can you say: "I am perfect as I am" – not with narcissism or when your ego is on a high – but with an open heart?

Indulging in addictive behaviour forms a routine that is useful for people who cannot process or deal with change. Addicts have come to believe that change is unsafe, so they devise a ritual to minimise their fear. Your habit stills the uncertainty – an uncertainty of which you might not even be aware – because you have lived unconsciously with it for so long that it has become how and who you are.

Chasing your tail

Watching someone in active addiction is like seeing a dog chasing its tail. They are going nowhere, but they are nevertheless experiencing the intensity of doing something. There is a fixation – like the dog focusing on its tail – but the entire exercise is in fact futile. It serves only as a distraction to pacify their relentless fear; the numb cycle continues and is self perpetuated.

All addicts are badly wired; their emotional security is misdirected. Possibly, they never learned to feel worthy of loving another or of being loved. However, they do manage to get attention from over-responsible others through their addiction, and this response serves a need. It is a pay-off. They have learned to manipulate others to care for them because they do not believe that they can find relationships in any other way.

You might say that life would be dull without an addiction – that addiction offers intensity and focus – and that an addicted individual is interesting because of these characteristics. However, addiction is not passion from the heart. It is a deep-seated anxiety from the head. Addicts will often attract other addicts, because they share a common yet unspoken understanding. Addicts need support and that is why they cluster together – it is for this same reason that a pain addict will draw in a persecutor. You will not be in a relationship with an addict unless you too have an addictive nature. This may be an addiction to fixing and solving other people's problems. An individual with a rollercoaster life full of highs and lows may generally find a consistent person boring, but may need them in a relationship because the consistent person will provide the external structure within which the addictive person can act out their addictions. An example of this would be an alcoholic who chooses an over-responsible (often referred to as co-dependent) partner to act as their caregiver. The partner will enable their out-of-control behaviour by providing a home base and a socially acceptable family environment. The structure supports the alcoholic's behaviour because it shields them from consequences that they would otherwise have had to face.

Creating friendships with other addicts also offers a unique form of community because you are unconditionally accepted within that group as you conform to that sort of lifestyle; you are a part of it and not apart from it. You have a home; a place where you belong and fit in – regardless of how dysfunctional your chosen home might be.

The positive aspect of addict gatherings are support groups in which people consciously decide to encourage each other to engage in healthy behaviour and to engage in uplifting, productive activities. This is where people who are prone to addictive behaviour can bond in hope instead of fear.

Negative bonding occurs when people group together to encourage addictive behaviour because they need to feel supported and justified in what they are doing. You are friends because you are at the same level of unconsciousness. Do you really trust these people? Do you trust yourself? It is well known that addicts lie. It is part of the deal. They are in denial of themselves to themselves – so other people inevitably also get caught in the sticky net of their deception. As an addict, you have roots with rot and you bond in fear.

The easiest way to overcome one addiction is to replace it with another. Can you transform your negative addictions into positive and productive ones? Are you willing to act out your compulsions for the greater good, or are you really enjoying your egocentric self-sabotage and the way in which you poison your environment?

At which temple do you worship? Where is it that you self-sacrifice? Is it at the Golden Calf Casino or the grey building where you light a candle to heat the spoon to stick the needle in? Is it at the incense house where you smoke your brains out, or at the funky sex club where you ritually queue for alcohol and flesh?

Do you accept that you will always have choice? You can choose to look at your insecurities, at how unable you are to engage in a healthy way with others. So why don't you choose this? Maybe it is too much hard work, and taking the easy route by sabotaging yourself and others seems more acceptable. Maybe you enjoy the pay-off that addiction brings you – being anaesthetised to pain and discomfort, and not having to take responsibility for your life. If you choose not to change, you must accept that the feeling you get from your addiction is simply more rewarding – for you – than love.

Living with an addict

The stark reality that one has to deal with is the fact that your relationship will never be the primary focus for your partner if your partner is an addict. You will always be sacrificed for the pay-off they get from their drug of choice. Nothing else is more important, especially when the person is in active addiction. There is a switch that jams and they no longer care about anyone except themselves, and they have no regard for the consequences of their behaviour. They are I-me-my-specialists. Ironically, you end up becoming obsessed with fixing their addictions. Addicts tend to display narcissistic behaviour – so when you make them your focus they get all the attention they desire.

However, they will expect you to help them when they come down off the high. The pattern is always the same. "So sorry … I am so embarrassed … it won't happen again." Until the next time. Eventually, they give up on the excuses and try other ways of pacifying your behaviour and justifying their own. Often they develop sneaky and devious ways of getting their fix and their behaviour becomes more secretive and filled with more lies. Do you want to live like this?

The Number One Rule is: Do not be over-responsible by enabling an addict's behaviour and the situation. When you enable an addict, you make it possible for them to continue their addiction. Do not make excuses for your partner who is unable to attend a social gathering unless inebriated. This is how the 'cover-up enabling strategy' begins. In the end you will be bailing the addict out of financial debt, making excuses for their absenteeism at work, and still putting up with abusive behaviour. Nothing that you can do will change anything. It is not your fault and it is not your problem. Addicts always need something or someone to blame. It is either the stress, or because you were not at home, or the children are noisy and badly behaved. The reasons are endless and they are very creative in coming up with them.

If you are in a relationship with an addictive type, you have two basic choices – stay in the relationship, or leave.

If you choose to stay in the relationship, what is it about this situation that draws you in and keeps you there? Maybe it looks like your childhood home environment. Why do you find this stressful situation acceptable? Maybe it is familiar and predictable – despite the chaos. Or maybe you understand it. Perhaps you are overly empathic and feel that the addict deserves the love that you should be giving to yourself. Where is your self-worth and where are your boundaries? You deserve better than this, don't you?

Being a crisis addict

Should you be attracted to this type of chaos, you may want to ask yourself if you know what stability looks like. If too much consistency and predictability cause some form of stress for you, it means that chaos is your comfort zone and peace is a stressor because it is the unknown. Living in a crisis situation may create meaning for you, and this gives you the misguided idea that you are actually in control and useful. Stress addicts often set unrealistic challenges and goals, and they create a pattern of stress-and-accelerate versus relax-and-brake. Speed up with stress, then release on a downhill – this is a recipe for hypertension. They need stress to get a feeling – to create a focus – and this focus is often outward in an attempt to avoid introspection.

Do you deliberately unhinge situations to cause chaos because you do not believe that peace can last? If you define periods in which there is no chaos as 'the calm before the storm,' this could indicate that you do not trust a stable environment. Maybe you are addicted to crises or to the emotional charges generated by crises; maybe you only feel valued and appreciated when you're fixing or managing a crisis; perhaps you're addicted to the sympathy and attention you get from other people when they hear about how much you're having to deal with; or maybe you are overly altruistic in your belief that you could show someone a better way of being.

Remember that the addict only finds meaning by romancing his or her addiction. Life is miserable without it. They do not see healing their addiction in a positive light – rather, they see it as something they have to 'give up'; they see it as a loss of something enjoyable. They do not consider the concept of 'gaining a life' by changing their self-sabotage paradigm.

We need to remind ourselves that being addicted to the chaos of another is very unsettling, and that this is not healthy. Staying in an environment of chaos will activate issues of rejection and loss – all the same issues you were forced to deal with as a child when you grew up in an unpredictable environment. You are recreating a circumstance that mimics your childhood in an attempt to fix something that is not fixable within your current relationship. You are not the scared child anymore, and you are dealing with a different person and a different set of circumstances now that you are an adult. Your current partner is not your parent.

It is pointless trying to work with the symptoms of your addiction. Rather deal with why you *again* choose to live in an environment that made you so very unhappy as a child. Therefore, if you choose to stay in this relationship, accept that this is how it is and how it will be for you. Your responsibility to yourself is finding the best way of managing your life within and around these circumstances of your choosing. When you find you are giving your power away to the drug – the abuser, the unchangeable – how do you reclaim your power?

Dealing with the feeling

What do you do when your addict-partner goes out and does not return at the time that they promised to return? And your phone calls are not being answered?

Let's look at an example. John and Mandy have decided to share their space and committed to a relationship together. John, however, has a habit of not honouring his side of the deal when he says that he will be home from work at a certain time – and then fails to arrive at the promised time. Mandy spends her time cooking a meal and waiting for John to return like he promised he would. Only later does she find out that John met his co-addict friend Andrew at a bar instead of going home as promised – John simply cannot tear himself away from the pseudo support and camaraderie that goes with a shared addiction. John chooses to prioritise his drinking relationship with Andrew over his commitment to his love for – and his relationship with – Mandy.

The primary response for most people is to personalise the situation:

- They have chosen to sit in the pub or casino without me – they don't care about me.
- Who are they with? In other words, how can they have fun with someone else and not me?
- Why didn't they tell me? You feel excluded from their enjoyable experience because you aren't a fellow addict.

It is worth noting that a person's addictive behaviour is usually not meant to be vindictive, nor is it directed at you. There is a switch that turns the addict into a self-indulgent, anaesthetised robot. They then move into a parallel universe – the one in which you do not exist because they have now become 'beside themselves.' They are not there as you would like to know them. There are often two or more personalities in there that the addict is not able to comfortably integrate. There is one face for you, and there are other faces for others.

Some addicts use their form of escapism to indirectly punish their partners. They may see their partner as the cause of certain unwelcome feelings – jealousy for example – that they are not able to control. They then choose to isolate themselves from the other because they may want to inflict pain on the one who destabilises their control. "You cause me feelings of inadequacy therefore I punish you by anaesthetising myself. I alienate myself from you because you hurt me."

To continue with the example – when John eventually does return home, he gets all the attention he wants. He becomes the centre of the conversation and the centre of Mandy's world. His feelings of inadequacy are satisfied because he can see how affected Mandy is by his behaviour. He can see her pain.

"We need to talk", says Mandy.

Yes, thinks John. Yes, let's talk about me! I want all your attention.

But instead he says, "What now? Don't tell me you're going to bring that up again. It's in the past. Get over it."

Ways of dealing

If you are feeling distressed and rejected, you have two behavioural options:

Rational:

- Get out of your emotions and into your head and consider your situation as if you were counseling someone else.
- Write down your feelings. Why do you want to take on their stuff? Try to practise releasing the fear-related issues of others. Do not share their fear burden with them.
- Look at reality. Know that it is not your fault and that nothing you do or do not do will change your partner's behaviour. It is their problem; let them have it.
- Analyse your options. Are you being over-responsible? How are you facilitating their addictive lifestyle?
- Do you deserve this lack of respect?
- Do you really want to live like this?
- Can you afford to become ill and emotionally exhausted by your partner's behaviour?
- Is it realistic that your emotions are governed by their behaviour?
- How much time and energy do you want to spend thinking about their pathologies?

Irrational:

- Emotional outburst – if you have an outburst, all the addict hears is white noise. No words reach their ears, just a crackling sound. So do not waste your energy and give them an excuse to blame you.
- You may find yourself creating your own perceived scenario of what the addict is doing, usually based on experience. This never works, it only increases your anxiety.

- You turn on yourself – maybe wanting to have a drink or take a tranquiliser as old baggage of loss and rejection from the past rears its head. Do not do this.
- You threaten to end the relationship, yet again. If you make threats, carry them out.
- You turn the situation in on yourself, thinking, "This is a personal attack on me. Why do I always end up with these types?" Yes, why do you?
- Plotting revenge – this is useless. You will only end up damaging yourself by doing things that are not in your nature, and you will end up disliking yourself.

It is important to allow yourself the space to address the feeling when it arises in the situation, and not to numb out and say you feel nothing. The sensation will be stored somewhere and you will either become ill and/or develop delayed anxiety because of it within the next few days. Know that addicts are a liability and as soon as you board the rollercoaster with them, you will be exposed to an up-and-down lifestyle that is bound to unsettle you.

You may say that you just cannot deal with the issue now because it is too much. Try to go the rational route and look at the bigger picture. It is not easy to be still and have clear thoughts during an emotionally disturbing and spun-out episode, but try to do something to change your environment.

- Either go for a drive to get out of your space or put on music that you find soothing.
- If it is safe, go for a walk near water or amongst a crowd.
- Write a letter to your partner and burn it.
- Make a list of the things that make you truly happy.
- Think about the ways in which you best express yourself.
- Have a bath in essential oils.

When you calm down, ask yourself these questions:
- Why does his/her behaviour have such a toxic effect on my emotions?

- Why have I attracted this situation into my life? What is my pay-off?
- Have I set a rewarding goal for myself?
- Am I aligned with myself?
- For whom am I living my life?
- How much time, attention and energy am I giving to this problem that I could be investing in myself?

Remember that you are not an extension of your partner – and vice versa. Is this kind of feeling really worth staying in the relationship for? If their behaviour is damaging your life and your self-worth – leave. You are not in this relationship to be a saviour or a counselor, nor should you stay in a relationship that damages you.

Often having one partner who is continuously riding the peaks and valleys of addiction will drive the other to becoming over-responsible. The consistent partner tries to soften the ride. This serves no healthy purpose, since the other gradually relinquishes all responsibility and you are blamed for their behaviour. Sit quietly and ask yourself the question, "Whose life am I really living; and do I fear living my life for me?"

Finally, if you cannot leave and nothing you try to do changes anything, it is time to surrender your situation to a Higher Power. Let go of your control and surrender. Stop trying to change your partner. Stop trying to work out why they lie to you, and why they betray you. You cannot be responsible for your partner's behaviour, but you can change your own behaviour. And in so doing your partner may choose to change their behaviour too.

Basic questions

"What are you doing with your life?" "What do you want to achieve in your short time on earth?"

You make the decisions that affect your life and there is nothing that you *have* to do. The next time you feel the need to stab someone with sarcasm, ask yourself, "What is really going on here? From what am I isolating and protecting myself?" Are you perhaps feeling compromised because you do not feel that you own your life? Do you feel you have no me-time and that you are constantly at the beck and call of others? Why do you feel the need to martyr yourself like this? Are you perhaps satisfying someone else's needs to have some need of your own fulfilled? What is this need? What is it that you fear losing by changing your behaviour and speaking your truth?

Do you give your partner the opportunity to grow up, or are you just picking up where their parents left off?

Sit with the feeling

Sit with the thought and the feeling. "How does this relationship work for me and how can I nurture the possibilities?" Do not indulge in behaviours that attempt to avoid feelings – such as drinking or gambling – to try to escape your emotions. Instead, welcome your emotions. You will be surprised how wonderful they can be once you make friends with them.

You can also take this opportunity to explore the more practical side of your relationship, for instance:

- Are the foundations of your relationship sound?
- Do you subscribe to the same intangible things, such as the same spiritual and moral principles?
- Do you both honour the importance of trust, respect and kindness within your relationship?
- What are your sharing habits?
- Are you both generous because you trust in the infinite abundance of the Universe, or does one of you live in fear of poverty and destitution? Remember that the rainy day never materialises. You just end up regretting what you did *not* do, not what you *did* do.
- Do you have similar backgrounds – therefore a common frame of reference? We have learned from our ancestors that it is easier to get along with someone in our environment if you share similar backgrounds. Try to simplify your life by having a close look at your relationships. There are enough other complications to deal with.

Be what you want

If you peel the pretentious gloss off society, it becomes evident that traditional roles have not intrinsically changed for thousands of years. Generally, women want gladiators who will fight for them and make them feel safe. Men want goddess admirers who stroke and nurture their egos. We should not, however, expect the 'James Bond syndrome' to be part of our experience. This is fiction – if something looks too good to be true, it most probably is. We need to accept our limitations and the limitations of others. We need to know that dreaming about leaving a current relationship because we think we will find a hero or a heroine to rescue us is just that – a dream.

However, what we can do is give each other more of what we wish to receive ourselves. Become more of what you want the other to be. If you desire more friendship, be more of a friend; if you want more love, be more loving. Be careful of creating fuzzy zones by saying, "You are the man and you should look after me and support me," followed by "Do you think you own me? I want to be respected as an independent person." Mixed messages cause confusion.

RITUALS AND CYCLES

ৎৡ৽ঔ

I bring to you the message of attunement ... to align yourself
with the rhythm of life and to appreciate all its cycles.

৵৽ঔ

Sadly, most regular ritual practice has been lost – particularly in modern Western society – since normal healthy systems broke down and living in communities with extended families became a thing of the past. Cultural rituals are useful in that they create order and harmony and give us a sense of belonging to a particular community. These rituals are the patterns that show us our place and our progress. We are safely inserted into the methodical cycles of the seasons and the moon by doing what has always been done – in this way rituals enable us to trust the process of our future with greater ease.

Prior to industrialisation we had to rely on ourselves and on one another for provisions, and so there was far more human contact than we have in modern society. There was a strong sense of community and items such as food, clothing, furniture and silverware were made locally. Life was hard because we were reliant on the weather for our crops, people generally did not earn much money, and they became ill and possibly died when epidemics spread though their villages. However, these circumstances encouraged a sense of humility in society as a whole. We turned to our Spiritual World for guidance and were comforted by friends and family in times of distress. Our lives had meaning because what we did was an extension of who we were; we had pride and we had purpose.

Industrialisation was the turning point. Power-driven machinery and mining for coal and iron became increasingly important, and eventually replaced home industries altogether. Division of labour was introduced to increase productivity and each worker was assigned one task. The shoemaker, who in the past had owned his shoe business, became part of the workforce, joined the factory line and was given the sole task of threading laces. Work became a repetitive and boring task in which one seldom saw the end product. Ultimately, when factories became the norm and the small home industries were forced to close down, people could not identify with their work because there was no ownership of it on any level. There was very little personal fulfilment and life became what Emile Durkheim referred to as 'the dull compulsion of being'.

The more advanced society became, the less need we had to interact on a personal level with each other, and our involvement in healthy rituals in our daily lives declined as a result. We lost our sense of belonging to a community and we found our egos.

Modern ritual

The most common Western ritual is the worship of materialism. Instead of acknowledging ancient symbols of wisdom, we collect modern symbols of status. We have to have ego-inflating devices such as the latest cell-phone, computer, or car – or whatever we think will make others stand back and look up to us. We choose materialism as our means of achieving admiration, and we believe that our possessions will fill the emptiness of having no real sense of belonging. In order to sustain this materialistic lifestyle, we surrender our spirituality and with that we surrender our cultural roots. These have all been replaced by corporate culture and ladder climbing. We have to get to the top of the ladder to be totally sure that there is nothing there. Listen to the voices of our *when-I* consciousness. It sounds something like this, "*When I* get that promotion, I'll be happy; when I lose this fat; when I find a good circle of friends".

Our elders – who used to be respected as wise counsellors – are worked out of the system because companies look at the bottom line and employ younger and cheaper labour. Unfortunately, there is no passion or emotional investment in working for a big corporate firm. As previously mentioned, prior to the industrial revolution home industry was the means whereby people earned their keep. These industries were handed down from one family member to the next through entire generations; and there was a certain amount of pride in what people did because it bore the family name. Their mode of income and their identity were rolled into one.

What are your daily rituals? Maybe you take the easy route and ritualise unhealthy behaviour. Instead of greeting the new day with meditation and peacefulness, you choose coffee and cigarettes. What do you do that makes you feel you belong, or do you already have a strong sense of being part of a bigger picture? Do you identify with the people in your neighbourhood and the country in which you live? Or do you ritualise 'home avoidance' by having drinks every day after work and wishing you were somewhere else, and with someone else?

Is the lack of healthy ritual in our society one of the reasons that there is such a marked increase in addictive behaviour and suicide? Are we all focussing on reality avoidance because we have lost our sense of belonging?

Ritual codes

Today, our ritual dress is the right designer label. Or we live in the right area and dine out at the right restaurant. We form insecure bonds by making lists of contacts to whom we send lots of spam mail and text message jokes – to remind them and ourselves that we still exist. Our ritual feasts are from the closest take-out and we eat fast food while we watch someone on television telling us who we are and how we should live and what to believe.

Why do we spend so much time in the zone of linear clock-watching and deadlines? No-one on their deathbed ever says they wish they had spent more time at the office. We generally do not make time in our lives to honour the rites of passage from childhood into adulthood, or from middle age to being anointed as a wise elder. The elderly are packaged into old age homes and pensioned off and the younger genera-tion typically do not consult their elders in times of crisis. We slide into adolescence and feel the pressure of our identity crises without support from our community, because everyone is too busy making money and thinking about making money to truly pay attention to anyone else around them. Soap operas then become our community and we end up believing that this how people live – and we even aspire to that.

Productivity and worthiness

Much of the stress we experience nowadays is caused by the perception that we have to be busy all the time. We sometimes rate our level of self-worth according to our degree of busy-ness. "Look how busy I am. I am so useful and therefore I have the right to live." We should consider viewing our year – from one birthday to the next – differently, for example by viewing it in terms of the changing seasons. When it is spring, we could be laying seeds and foundations; in summer the seeds continue to grow; in autumn we can harvest our crops; in winter the land lies dormant in preparation for the next year's crop, and we slow down too.

So what do we do now that we've figured out that being busy all the time comes at a price? What do we turn to now that all our community rituals have been erased? We create our own addictive ways of life. Adolescence is very often the time in our lives that addictive behaviour starts because of the identity crisis we experience at this stage of our development. Ideally, this transformation from childhood to adulthood happens within a structured environment. Most people need rules to feel comfortable at this stage of their lives, because adolescence is a time of feeling lost and needing a safe structure within which to experiment with who we are.

Does modern society offer us that freedom and that safety? Can parents make the time to nurture and facilitate this phase of their children's lives when they are burdened with their own baggage as adults? Unfortunately, if the teenager's immediate family is not interested and not listening, the adolescent will likely look elsewhere for a community to which they can belong. Adolescents will find acceptance and affirmation in other areas with other people. If there were elders available, the younger people could have turned to them for wisdom and non-judgemental support.

LOVE STYLES AND MARKETING STRATEGIES

I bring you the message of discernment ... to find out what you feel.
You will be reminded that there is more than one kind of love.

Love styles

Hendrick *et al* (1986) elaborated on the different ways in which people behave within interpersonal relationships. They defined six Love Styles and gave them each a unique Greek name.

- *Eros* – This style represents passionate love where lovers describe how they were immediately attracted to one another. Passionate love often seems too emotional to be indefinitely maintained and may last best when the fantasy of it is not laid out into the light of reality.
- *Storge* – This style is used to describe companionate love; a deep friendship between two people who share a lot in common and who care for and respect one another.
- *Ludus* – This style is used to represent game-playing love. Love becomes a manipulative dance in which the issue, "I don't know where I stand in this relationship," becomes a common concern.
- *Mania* – This style is an overly possessive kind of love. An individual acting out this style will feel agitated and tense if he or she suspects that their partner is with someone else.

- *Pragma* – This is the logical love style. A relationship develops if he or she fits into the social norms, structures and values of a given culture. Both parties come from the same background and their relationship seems a logical choice. It fulfils many of the practical aspects within a relationship.
- *Agape* – This style is representative of selfless love and a person expressing this style would rather suffer themselves than have their lover suffer.

Some interesting information has emerged from various studies done in the area of love styles. Women who scored high in possessive love also experienced high levels of verbal and physical aggression within their relationships (Bookwala *et al*, 1994). People who are very invested in themselves and their need to be independent, demonstrated game-playing love as their most prominent style (Dion *et al*, 1991). The Ludus interpersonal relationship style is regarded as the least satisfactory relationship style, as it leads to multiple partners, loneliness, and unhappy relationships (Hensley, 1996).

Phases of relationship

It is good to be aware that relationships, as living things, have phases. In the first three weeks, you will normally share some amazing times and a rare bad moment and then decide that you are either ready – or not – for a more serious commitment. You will either settle for "Let's just be friends," or you may say, "Where to from here?" When one partner wants the relationship to continue and the other does not, you may settle for a sex-buddy agreement – just to see what happens, or maybe just to avoid being alone.

At three months, the first mask starts to slip. Some of the little things that you were not too sure about begin to surface more often. You may wonder where the person you met went to.

At six months, all the masks are off and you either really enjoy each other's company or you get into a habit because everyone invites you out together and you have become used to a certain shared routine. You may hear yourself saying "Better the devil you know..." and feel that it is too much effort to start all over again with someone new. But you are actually disappointed that all the potential you saw in the beginning of the relationship has not emerged.

At 30 months, your hormones and the fantasy have fallen flat and there really are no palpitations or sweaty palms left in the relationship. If you have a good, solid friendship your relationship will glide through this stage. If things have been a bit rocky for a few months prior to this turning point, your relationship will most likely end. However, if you both choose to address your issues and obstacles, the relationship has a good chance of surviving past this point. If you work together, you can turn your relationship around.

Relationship marketing strategies

Do you view a relationship as a kind of deal you decide to get involved in, and if so, why? Do you make mental notes when you meet someone, weighing up whether they have enough to offer you? You may even think, "He is a real bargain..."

Viewing a relationship in this light is highly paradoxical because things of the heart cannot be traded. They are an extension of our personal truth and of our ability to love ourselves. But the world in which we play and live is a material one and it is seen as normal to succumb to the agenda of measuring the people we become involved with at the expense of being real.

If you choose to present yourself as a product, there are various ways in which you can promote yourself to draw someone in. Sometimes we use strategies that we have seen working for others and sometimes we try out new ones for ourselves. The focus is usually on how the new relationship will make us feel. "Will this package deal satisfy my agenda?" Occasionally this strategy can benefit both parties in a relationship, but this seldom happens because both will probably be acting from a point of insecurity.

We style our self expression on one or more of the four broad dimensions of our make-up – spiritual, physical, intellectual, and emotional. Some will conform to one dimension only; others will use several in combination. The dimension that we favour depends on what we have come to believe works best for us and the situations in which it has the greatest effect and the biggest pay-off for us.

All relationship marketing strategies are based on a need to achieve and a need to please. They are not the authentic behaviour of an individual. There is a clear difference between someone whose intentions and behaviour are real and someone whose design is structured on being a fake. An authentic individual is real; they know who they are and are able to express their true selves in any environment. A fake person is a variant of another personality; they are a replica of someone else whom they admire, or a person they would like to be.

Spiritual strategy

Some people choose to use spirituality as a strategy. This approach to spirituality is very often based on books they have read or things they have heard or learned. They studied 'how to be spiritual' – all words and no heart – but are nevertheless very good at reciting texts and offering advice. The concept of soul mates or twin souls will probably come up in the conversation. You will have found each other – your other half; your meaning in life. These people will be able to regurgitate phrases from Buddhism or other spiritual teachings that may make you feel that you are fortunate to find someone who is so 'connected'. They are not like all the others. Or are they? Evaluate this individual's life realistically. Do they back up their words with actions?

How do they spend their time? What are their interests? Do they want to move in with you because they have nowhere else to stay at the moment? Or perhaps they are chronically between jobs and between relationships waiting for someone else to provide for them. Are these people true to themselves, or is the so-called spiritual leader just a con in a kaftan?

Physical strategy

Or maybe we choose to style our self expression based on the physical. This strategy is less subtle than people who base their sense of self on concepts of spirituality. Consider how we use our dress code to attract others. How do you dress when you are going out, when your thoughts are focused on finding 'the one' or finding someone else whose attention you seek? Do you use clothing that you think will draw someone in, and if so – why do you presume to know that it will attract anyone in particular?

It is generally accepted that sex sells, so the physical strategy with the highest returns will certainly be sexual in nature. The more of your physical self you can expose to someone else, the greater you assume your chances are of attracting the other. Using this tactic can be hard to maintain within a relationship, because it is severely limiting. You limit yourself to being a mere physical entity. Until your shelf life expires. And because the type of person you entertain on the physical level will only want what you promoted, you will be expected to deliver the goods. Note that this is a popular and easily attainable means to an end, so there will be plenty of competitors out there vying for someone's attention based on what they look like. Do you have anything different and better to offer?

Look at your current relationship and examine your dress code. How were you dressed when you met your partner? Did you change your clothing to attract him or her? Over a period of time you may start feeling insecure within your relationship because you are not generating the same effect in the other like you used to. Do you then revert to your initial strategic behaviour – even unconsciously?

As time passes, it may become tiresome to maintain the mating-game dance. When he wants you to wear a bunny suit or do a pole dance "Like you used to do in the beginning", you may find that your interest has waned. You have moved on to a point in the relationship where you're no longer interested in engaging with the world in a purely physical way. It is simply not appropriate – for you – anymore. You have grown up. Yet he is stuck and needs that form of affirmation to prove his worth and to feed his ego. It worked in the beginning after all…

Consider how much of your emotional identity you invest in role playing and the costumes that you wear. If you deviate from that script, expect a response.

"I don't know you like this."

And you could say. "You don't even know who I am".

And you would both be right because neither of you have ever told or shown the other who you really are. You marketed the wrapper and now you expect the other to understand the contents.

Intellectual strategy

If you decide not to use the spiritual or physical dimensions to express who you are, you might resort to using your intellect. The intellectual strategy is fairly polarized. On one hand, there is the quasi-intellectual idiot who thinks he knows everything and gives you his business card before you have exchanged names. You are meant to feel intimidated by his incredible card, but he wants you to see his title because that is all he is. It is always useful to ask, "And besides this, what is it that you do with your life?"

There are also those who have always had a bigger and better experience than anyone present. She has done it all and can explain everything because she is the only one who can sort out the world's problems. These people pride themselves on delivering the goods; they are the only ones who can bring a project to deadline. And they will say they never flirt because they either do not know how to or because it is too trivial. But they do. It is never overt, though. They play an intellectual sparring game and subtly remind you that they have just that little bit more to offer than the airhead over there. "I may not have the looks, but hey, I've got so much more to offer than that bimbo."

On the other hand, there are true intellectuals whose focus is very much more on gathering information than on collecting relationships. But more often than not these intellectuals enjoy playing around in the academic playground. Often, because most of life's attention has been cerebral, the heart space is neglected and you may find an interesting trend emerging: the higher the IQ, the lower the EQ (emotional intelligence). Also, the affair or relationship should ideally slot in with their academic pursuits and their schedule since they like having their egos stroked now and again.

Emotional strategy

Those who use the emotional strategy to express their self worth are most often women, but not always. These women play the 'woe is me' role very well. They want help and support because the world is harsh and stressful and they need someone who is strong and able to protect them, and to rescue them from everything, including themselves – because they are victims.

"I try so hard, but the minute I get myself sorted out and life is going smoothly another bullet comes and shoots me down."

The rescuer will come and pick up the pieces and put them together again and will feel empowered by the other's apparent disempowerment. However, if the needy one wakes up and becomes self-sufficient, the needed one will have a crisis because their role will have ended. Redundancy means it's time to find another job and another cause. It is therefore good to remember that there is no such thing as a free lunch. If you are looking for someone to support you financially, know that this comes with a standard pair of golden handcuffs.

Finding the fit

We need to remember that when a strategy is involved, both parties will be playing an active role. One partner does the marketing and the other falls for the product. They find a 'fit' with one another. People do and say the things that they know others will want to see and hear. Whatever you project into the environment will be attracted to you and vice versa. Remember to take note of the actions of people and not only their words. It is easy to be cerebral in a relationship and to conceptualise the theory of 'perfect' oneness. Yet following through and being true to one's intentions and aspirations while retaining an open heart can be more difficult than it seems.

If you were attracted to someone's strategy and find it to be a mask, you need to make a choice. There will usually be more than one personality in there to suit different occasions. Can you live with that? Only if someone demonstrates consistent behaviour over a wide range of social engagements will you know that they are authentic.

Also look to what it is that you are doing that may not be authentic, since this behaviour will draw in more of the same. If one person in the act changes roles, this change affects the other and quite often makes them put on a new mask. Both people involved in the game need to examine their behaviour to understand why they choose to play roles with each other instead of feeling worthy enough to be real.

And you hear a voice saying:

"I don't want you to change. I want you to be the person I thought you said you were."

And you wonder who that is...

GETTING TOGETHER

❧❦

The minute I heard my first love story, I started looking for you, not knowing how blind that was. Lovers don't finally meet somewhere. They're in each other all along.
– Maulana Jalalu'ddin Rumi

❧❦

In the beginning was the Glue

What was your role modeling like when you were growing up? Perhaps your parents showed you how to build a healthy and happy relationship and presented you with a real-life example of what a healthy relationship can be like. How many wounds do you have and how far are you in your healing process? How do you choose the person with whom you wish to be bonded and what was the glue that you first used to bind yourself to this other?

- Where did your relationship start?
- What drew you in?
- Who were you when you met?
- What were your circumstances at that time?

How well have you glued together all the experiences through your formative years – all the times that you felt as if you were disintegrating and falling into little pieces? Each of these cracks holds a memory – a weak spot – which under pressure will remind you of how fragile you are. It is very often our woundedness that draws us to another because we recognise similar cracks within their shell. And we want to fix the cracks in others instead of fixing them in ourselves first.

An individual who has paid attention to their cracks and consciously filled them with care, is more likely to make an emotionally wise decision when entering into a relationship. Someone who has lived in denial and neglected their wounds by suppressing and ignoring their emotional flaws is more likely to make an immature choice when looking for a partner. They will look for a relationship to fill a gap where they feel something is missing. Is it not perhaps yourself that you seek?

Consider these three scenarios and see whether you relate to any of them.

Scenario 1

Sally had reached a point in her life where she wanted a husband and children. Not only were most of her friends married, but her family was also pressurising her to settle down. When she met Steve at a product launch, she felt she had found what she had been waiting for. He was a successful businessman, educated and independent and had spent most of his time focusing on his career. The idea of a family appealed to him somewhat. It made him socially more acceptable and this would promote his career interests. She would provide the home and raise the children and he would be the head of the house. The initial glue between them was based on how the 'package' of family life would suit their individual aspirations. Over time, however, Sally realized that he did not love her the way she expected he would and Steve was often away at meetings or functions while she sat at home with the children. She got what she wanted, but not in the way she had expected. The suburban-dream glue had cracked.

Scenario 2

When Pierre met Billy at a friend's party, he thought he had met his soul mate. He had been doing months of introspection and reflection and Billy seemed just fabulous and so interested in learning from him. Billy, however, loved to party and had stored some 'soul words' but he was really taken with Pierre's depth and intensity. And besides being quite sexy, Pierre seemed so different from all those other superficial clubbing types – he felt as if he'd known Pierre forever. Billy wanted to explore that 'other side' of himself; to be with someone who could tell him how to find himself. They spent the whole evening together exchanging ideas and stories. A few months later, however, Billy was out partying again. The deep stuff just wasn't working for him and Pierre was disappointed at Billy's fickleness. He thought Billy would become his soul mate. The fantasy-counselor glue had melted.

Scenario 3

Karen and Elaine met at a walking club. Karen loved the outdoors and after her last relationship ended, she joined a group of people who gathered to take walks in nature. Elaine's marriage had been disastrous. Based on the remnants of an unhappy marriage and other experiences, Elaine decided that men were out of her life forever. She and Karen chatted about their hurt and their past disappointments on their walks together, and Karen took Elaine under her wing. They would be there for each other and she would show Elaine the way. The idea of being nurtured and understood really appealed to Elaine – she felt rescued and accepted. Maybe this was what she had been missing all the time? As time passed, Elaine found Karen too smothering. She needed space and wasn't sure what she wanted in terms of a relationship. The pain-rescue glue of their relationship had dissolved.

Pain glue

Did you bond in pain? If so, the relationship will be glued in unhappiness. If you were both on the rebound, your relationship will be double-glued that way because both of you were looking to the other for reassurance, affirmation, and completion.

If you are still in the process of mourning the loss of a relationship, your wounds will be open and raw. The person you assumed was there for you has rejected remaining in relationship with you, and you feel a sense of loss and abandonment as a result. This trigger can fling you back into childhood and your heartache will be intense – you have been reminded of your deepest childhood fears: rejection and abandonment. This situation can leave you feeling small and afraid and lost; feelings that you may have had as a little child when you felt neglected or invisible. Then, with this emotional child crying within you, you seek out someone to rescue you; someone to fill the void and to save you. You simply do not want to be single now, although it would be better in the long term if you did nurse and heal yourself before investing in a relationship just yet. There are times in our lives when we really do need to lick our own wounds.

Rescue glue

You may possibly delegate someone else to be your counselor; your saviour. Over time, you will expect them to play that role in the relationship. When they are down and in need of your help, you will not cope because they are meant to be strong for you. That is why you chose them. If you are bonding with another in order for them to make you feel whole, you are doing it for the wrong reasons. They cannot pick up the pieces for you and make it better. And you have no right to give them that responsibility.

However, you may not have been dumped – you may just need to be in a relationship, either because you do not like being single, or because everyone you know has a partner. This need overrides all rational thinking, and you may find yourself sacrificing much of yourself just to be bonded to someone else; anyone else. This need is your glue and later you could find yourself resenting not doing things for yourself, or you might feel that you are not appreciated. Yet you fear losing the other so intensely that you stay stuck in your current relationship.

Sex glue

If your relationship was based on a strong sexual attraction, you will default to the same circumstances to feel worthy during a time of relationship stress. You will play the sex games that you needed to play to feel worthy in the initial phase of the relationship. Your sense of maintaining your position within your relationship will be reflected in what was laid down in the beginning because the cracks show when we are under strain; when things go wrong.

Do you hear your partner saying, "We always used to do this", "You always used to be more of that"? In other words, they are saying that your presence *'like that'* in the relationship used to define their way of relating to you, and that you're no longer doing it – whatever 'it' may be. This means that they've outgrown you; they've lost interest in you. They are not supporting the self-worth that you initially gained by making their ego your responsibility. "You never initiate anything sexual … I always have to do everything."

Common glue

Where was your relationship born – at a bar, a club or a party? Or maybe at a photography class, in the workplace, or at an art course? Was it this common ground that initially attracted you to your partner? Shared interests generally do provide us with a foundation for understanding one another because we have something to discuss or to do together. The venue you were at and the mood you were both in at the time of your first meeting will determine how you got to know one another initially. The part of yourself that you chose to expose to the other will be your first impression and vice versa. We often hear that first impressions are lasting impressions. But are they? And if they are, how long do they last?

If you later discover that your partner was attending a course or was at a club only to meet people, you may find that the common ground was actually a mirage; a means to an end and not an interest. It worked for a while but was not sustainable because it was unauthentic behaviour. If there is no substance behind the personality you met, there will be little left to keep you glued together later and you may find, eventually, that the glue becomes a sticky mess.

Our relationships are defined by the circumstances and the level at which they were created. Look at your experiences and circumstances at the time that you started this relationship. We often use a relationship to divert attention away from other issues; especially if there is an unwillingness or an inability to form a respectful, loving relationship with ourselves. Bonding through selfish neediness creates unrealistic expectations both of oneself and of the other. We must always bear in mind that problems later on in the relationship can only be resolved at the level at which they were created.

What is the binding glue in your current relationship? What is your historical glue? Do you stick to your partner because:

- You fear rejection or loss,
- You are pacifying feelings of insecurity and inferiority,
- You lack your own identity,
- You have no personal focus in your life,
- Your relationship suits your circumstance.

The primary ingredients of the glue are the substances that you put into your initial marketing strategy.

- What was the glue you used when you met?
- What was your greatest need at that time?
- Who was the person on whom you put your glue in the past – and would you choose to glue to this person today?

Fantasy and relationship

The one

What does 'the one' actually mean and when did you first start creating the concept of this fantasy person? We are all introduced to fairy tales like Cinderella and Sleeping Beauty as children, but the adults reading them to us forget to remind us that they are fiction. So we remember … if you are a beautiful and desperate princess trapped in a tower you will be rescued by a gallant prince with status and money. It is a fantasy that we cling to when we are young to give us hope that we will one day be loved unconditionally; that we will be good enough. The perfect one will find us and see through all our masks and rescue us. We will live happily ever after.

However, in the real world, everyone with whom you choose to have a relationship will offer you exactly the same as you're getting right now because of who you currently are. Relationships may start off with the perfect dance and pretentious impressions, but they all end up with the same issues. Only when you decide that you want to engage differently will you find someone different. Do not give up on one relationship and think that you will find someone better – especially if *you* are still the *same*. There is also no point in living in fear of committing to someone because the 'right one' might appear soon after you commit to the 'wrong' person. Natural law dictates that you will draw the same messenger into a relationship over and over again; they just have different faces. Learn your lesson first and only then will you be free to move on and attract someone different.

We have relationships with the people around us so that we can teach – as well as learn from – one another. The relationship you are currently in is as good as it gets for who you are NOW. Your partner reflects your behaviour as well as what you are unconsciously asking for. Whatever you project out into your environment will be drawn towards you. If you want 'the one', you too have to become 'the one' by being at one with yourself.

The truth is that the fantasy person you are looking for is actually YOU; your Higher Self who is your soul connection to the Higher Power. You have to learn to love yourself before you can love another. You have to be what you want – so be loving and you will be loved in return.

Addiction to a fantasy world

The creation of a fantasy world starts out in childhood and adolescence when we drift towards creating a perfect person with whom to have a relationship – in our minds. Because of a lack of nurturing from our environment, we needed another world to live and love in. The person we chose to create then was perfect in every way and we had total control over all the circumstances and emotions in our fantasy with them. We owned the other person, we owned the situation as well as the happily ever after.

In the real world when you meet someone, you may insert them into your highly developed fantasy world. However, they are a real person to whom you have given life in your dreams. When the fantasy becomes a reality and the person does 'unfantasy' things, it all becomes too harsh and the dream ends. You feel disappointed because the idealised fantasy you had of the person is not congruent with who they really are. They have become another person, like you. This person has to be deleted because they could not sustain the perfection of your dreamworld. You will have to move on and find a real fantasy-perfect person. Sometimes we need to be reminded that we are human and there are no perfect princes and princesses out there.

Authentic fantasy

Ironically, we want others to be authentic – but when they are we reject them because they never match up to our fantasy. And then we need to try another person, because they could be 'the one'. We become addicted to the possibility of living out our fantasy by finding a love object and obsessing about them. This creates a high because of the potential of getting close to that perfection. Our entire focus is directed towards the possibility of engaging with this person and the fantasy is usually sexual and physical. Very often after a conquest, the love object is dropped and broken because once reality sets in there is usually disappointment accompanied by a low. And then the cycle starts again ... avoid reality ... new fantasy ... a cycle of roller-coaster addiction.

Sometimes the love object then decides to become unavailable to the addict and the hunt can resume. Usually the addict will drop the love object when they find another fix of interest who can give them a better feeling. We become addicted to the unpredictability of changing fantasies because we have programmed these imagined fantasies as our safety zone.

Choosing true relationship

Are you looking for completion of yourself in another? Or have you truly found the end of your love-partner journey? This will depend entirely on your relationship with yourself, and whether your heart is open or closed – to yourself and to the world. An open heart-space will allow you to experience every possibility more freely and with more love – for yourself and for others.

Soul truth

If you live and love with an open heart, you will not find yourself standing in a position of judgment of good versus bad before deciding to commit to a relationship. You would not have made lists weighing up the pros and cons of what you want, neither would you analyse or scrutinise the other. You will have stopped living in your head and started feeling with your heart. Only when you are at a place in which you unconditionally accept another as they are without fear of losing yourself, are you ready for a soul emotional investment. This is the glue that will set and keep you together – the other becomes part of you, but still remains apart from you. The glue that binds you is moulded in truth, and you are together out of choice – not desperation or neediness. And you will choose to be together for as long as the love lasts.

Warning bells

Warning bells must sound, however, if someone instantly wants to commit to you or if they make promises of 'forever after' shortly after meeting you. Especially those who tell you that they feel they have known you their whole life and maybe in another life too. The chances are high that they have addictive natures and that they need instant gratification derived from the feeling they get from the intensity of a new relationship. He may have said, "I noticed you right across the room and when our eyes met, I just knew." He saw in you what he wanted and needed to complete his life. Take an honest view of this person's relationship history before leaping into and committing to this one. Of course love at first sight does happen – just be sure that your eyes and heart are wide open when it does.

Open eyes

Sometimes, the person you really could share your life with is right under your nose, but you are not ready to see them – yet. You may still be trapped by your insecurities and may unconsciously be repeating the same type of self-sabotaging relationships because that is the only way you know how to relate to another. It is your habit. When you no longer need the thrill of the hunt or the chase, or the sweaty palms and palpitations, you will be able to see clearly who is essentially good for you. When you are truly in alignment with yourself and you feel worthy of giving and receiving love – then you will find the person with whom you could share your life.

Meeting the family and friends

Do you get worried at the stage of a relationship when you're expected to meet your partner's friends and family? Why is this? Although it is not a good thing to judge someone by their family, it is helpful to be aware of where and how they were raised and trained.

Sometimes we feel that we will be criticised for our choice of partner, that we will be judged. We can hear our family say, "She is not top drawer; not one of us," or "Why on earth do you think this relationship will work?"

Foundations

Your early learning will lay the foundation for what makes you feel comfortable when interacting with your partner's family and friends. If, over the years, you heard your family making derogatory comments about certain types of people, it will instil in you the idea that this 'type' is not suitable for you. This doesn't mean that this is right or wrong, it just is that way.

We all grow up in different families within different groups – with different norms and values and cultures. Sometimes we even have different mother tongues. You will know when entering someone else's home whether you feel you belong or not. How they dress, how they eat, how they relate to one another, and how their day is ritualised – such things will tell you this. As soon as you put yourself in an environment that feels uncomfortable, it will create stress because of the compromises that you feel you need to make, as well as perceived pressure to accommodate and adapt to the situation. There can also be feelings of resentment, because it becomes clear to you that the ways of your family are not honoured within the relationship.

Tolerance and understanding are great universal principles when applied globally, but a relationship is difficult enough without having to factor those variables into your day-to-day life.

If you feel that introducing your partner to your family and friends may be a problem, it probably will be. That is your clue. You can say, "It's not fair, my family don't like her", but in time, there will probably be things that she does that do irritate you, and you might not understand why this is happening to your relationship.

Good friends can be very objective advisors, and they will see things that you could miss when you are on cloud nine. Bad friends are usually unhappy when you are happy so their input should not count. Seeing your partner interact with their friends will give you a good idea about their ability to interact with others – as well as the type of person they feel comfortable with. The fact that your partner is willing to share their friendships with you is a good sign.

The exceptional ones

We must, however, not dismiss those relationships that do work against all odds. These are the exceptions. That is why we take note of them. We read their stories and say, "This is amazing and special. They must really love each other!"

GAMES AND OTHER FORMS OF MANIPULATION

I bring to you the message of centredness... to have the will to listen to your heart and to release your fears.

Everybody plays the game

Most games consist of a contest with rules and are usually played over a specific time-frame. We normally play games for entertainment and interaction with others; they are a past-time.

If we take the game of poker as an example, we will see that there are rules, a specific language, as well as the tools for playing the game.

Let's consider the following example. Around 52 people are invited to attend a party and as they start to mingle, David checks Denise with his poker-face; he doesn't like to show his emotional intent. But he isn't the only one who is interested in playing. Mark feels that he has a full house to offer, and decides to place a bet on Denise. Meanwhile, Daniel calls her from across the room and puts in his two-cents' worth. Mike, the joker, then decides to rise to the occasion and steps in to distract Denise from her conversation with Daniel. Denise, however, thinks it's all a big bluff and decides to fold – and so Jane enters the game.

Who plays these games – and do they serve a purpose? Who really wins and takes home the pot?

Games can be likened to training and it is interesting to note who the trainer is in a relationship. It's like going to puppy school – one person teaches the tricks and the other waits for treats.

There are many different love games we can play and they are all based on being unauthentic. At one stage or another, most of us have been seduced into playing a game – either consciously or unconsciously.

Just being on the list

Consider a very popular game that entails keeping someone on a list of willing and available playmates; these playmates are then taken out and put back into the toy box when it suits the player. If you are one of these toys in the game, ask yourself if you enjoy waiting for those unpredictable calls and whether you really feel worthy and respected by this person who messes with your heart?

You may recognise the following text message from someone you see from time to time, "I miss you, where are you now?" The purpose of this message is to keep you hanging in; the sender wants to stay top of your mind. The message, put more honestly, reads: "Don't forget me because I want you to always be available in case I need you. I want you to drop everything that you are doing now and accommodate me." The goal of the game-player is to train a team of playmates who will play uncommitted and uncomplicated games. The playmates become conditioned by this other person to wait for little snacks every now and then. The trainer would want you to validate their position by sending a return message saying that you are always available; and they may then let you know that you responded just a little too late. And so you are kept waiting for the next text-treat.

Realistically, these list collectors certainly do not miss you enough to attend a social function with you because, firstly, that means 'going public' and this could compromise their single status; the rule is that the relationship is a private affair. Secondly, it means that the control over the game is lost, because the venue and the rules have changed and they are kept waiting for what they want from you. In other words, you are compromising the game and they do not have 'home base advantage'. If someone is only willing to see you on their terms and calls you in the late evening – or night – to ask you if you miss them because they are waiting for you, or they just happen to be around the corner, what do you think they want from you? Do you really think you are the only person they called? What reserve number on the dating game list are you?

You need to take a serious look at this type of relationship circumstance and consider where it is that you learned to engage in this type of relationship – and why you do this to yourself. Are you carrying old stuff from the last experience or is this game unique to your current relationship? What are you acting out, or who is acting out their stuff on you? Have games honestly worked for you in the past, and how did they work? Did you benefit from assuming another role? And who really wins?

Your win: short-term high.

Your loss: self-esteem.

Hide and seek

Another type of game people play in relation to the other is hide-and-seek. In this game, the distance pursuer needs an external focal point of intensity when relating to others – so they decide to create a dance around their hearts. "You step this way and I'll step that." It is a ducking and diving game of hide-and-seek, which aims to keep feelings out of the way. The relationship is placed outside of the self so that you do not have to take responsibility for any emotional involvement. Maybe relationships are generally too boring for you, and playing cat and mouse keeps you on the edge and excited. Or maybe relationships let you down in other ways and speak to your unresolved loss and abandonment issues.

Your win: you think you are safe.

Your loss: you remain beside yourself.

The silent act

Others play elusive games by withholding information. They are secretive about who they are, and sometimes we find ourselves drawn into the mystery of what we think is lurking behind the closed door. We want to know more about this person, but know that if we start questioning, it would not be appreciated. They could get up and leave saying, "I don't need all this heavy stuff. Just chill out." This means that they have no interest in sharing anything with you. Often, however, they are quite empty and there simply is nothing in there to share.

Your win: there is someone in your life.

Your loss: time and energy.

The already-married

A relationship with someone who is already married can also result in game-playing because of all the false promises and maybes. The married one wants it both ways – they want the pretence of slotting into the social norm, and they want you for their 'other' entertainment. If you hear comments about the married person's partner such as, "We don't even speak anymore. They sleep on their side of the bed and I sleep on mine; our toes don't even touch," ask yourself why they still choose to live there. Why is she waiting for the children to finish school; or why is he hanging in until his job promotion is finalised; or are they both waiting for the other to make the first move out of the house? It takes courage to grow a spine and to stop making excuses; to be honest with oneself, one's family and with the other person in the relationship.

Some people pacify their feelings of rejection by chatting up other people's partners because they think that those people's partners will not view them as a threat. Often, this is how people have vicarious relationships and how they get attention. By being involved everywhere and committing nowhere, and thereby having a life of infinite pretend-possibilities that seem to be so much safer than real commitments.

What is it that you hope to gain by being involved with someone who is already committed? Does the arrangement suit you – and if so, why? Be prepared to say what it is that you want and look at reality, not at the dream. You are enabling another's committed relationship; the energy you invest and the entertainment you provide by spending time with the married one helps to maintain their public relationship.

Your win: some affection and attention.

Your loss: self worth.

Hard-to-get

If you take on the role of hard-to-get, you need to be reminded that this type of game is just that: it is a game, not a relationship. Why do you do it? Do you want to keep someone available, but not close enough to allow them to get to know you? Maybe you just want to pacify your ego by seeing who will jump through a ring of fire for you – just for kicks. Perhaps you want to experiment with how much someone will do for you, and how fast they will run to keep up with you.

"Let's see how much attention I can get or how many gifts I can collect if I play hard to get."

"How many admirers can I entertain if I keep my options open by having many irons in the love fire; if I lead them all on by acting available and interested?"

Why do you need someone to prove their affection for you? Is it because you do not trust your own ability to sustain your affection for another, or do you possibly feel undeserving of their affection?

Your win: you think you're in control.

Your loss: you're not in control.

People who play games can easily lose themselves in their created characters until life becomes one big act. Ultimately, games cannot last forever without causing the player harm. It is in our human nature to yearn to love and be loved. That is really why you are playing after all, isn't it?

YOU

Reflecting on wins and losses to your emotional status quo

Invitation to join a love game

Time expires: Game over

Both playing fun and games

Both have different goals and start playing mind games

Are you the same after the game? Have you learned more techniques to enable you to play a better game next time? Have you realised that there are no winners in love-games?

Negative behaviours

Criticism and control

Why do people in a relationship criticise each other? Ironically, this is the person with whom you chose to share your life and your space, so by running them down you are saying, "I am no good at making correct choices for myself."

In the real relationship world this tends to happen over time – especially as those unspoken things fester and grow. If we don't express issues that concern us or discuss circumstances that make us feel uncomfortable, they build up and we could end up being filled with doubt and mistrust of the other. Often we can end up creating scenarios that don't exist because we have misunderstood situations and have not asked for clarification.

One of the primary reasons for criticising the other is that we feel undervalued, excluded or taken for granted. We take this as a subtle form of rejection, which results in our taking our feelings of insecurity out on the other. Ultimately, we are both chipping away at the other's self-esteem and clipping each other's wings.

Criticism from one about the other often occurs because your significant one is not responding *emotionally* in the way that you would like them to. Critical remarks therefore become separated from your actual need for affection, and emerge as other behaviours. You may feel excluded from aspects of their life and interpret this as rejection. Your reactions are in response to your feelings of invisibility as you perceive your partner as being absent. You feel you are given no place in the important aspects of their life. You start to lay down rules for your own emotional safety, and your behaviour changes because you no longer feel open and caring towards your partner. However, if your partner were loving and kind towards you, they could act out the same behaviour and you wouldn't make critical remarks. It is important to let people be who they are without it evoking a fear response within you.

If you look at the total relationship behaviour – both yours and that of your partner – objectively and see it as unacceptable, make your point as you would with a person with whom you are not emotionally involved. Do not take their behaviour as a personal attack on yourself because, if you do, you will constantly be surrendering your emotional stability.

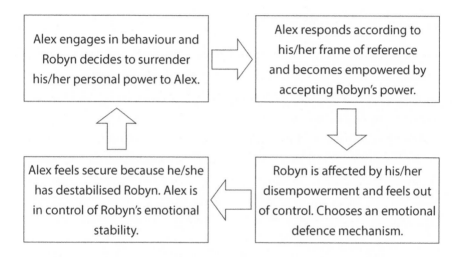

Intercept this downward spiral in the beginning by asking yourself if your response is rational or irrational. Communicate your true feelings and review why their behaviour has such a profound effect on your emotional stability and why you willingly surrender your personal power.

Constructive criticism versus manipulation

Constructive criticism is generally a valid and balanced opinion of another. Both positive and negative comments are seen as appropriate in a relationship, and they are given with good intent. However, criticism is harmful if it is used as a means of control and manipulation; the intent is bad and only serves to erode a relationship, and each other's self-esteem, over time. People often use guilt as a tool for manipulating another.

Consider this example of guilt manipulation in a relationship. A couple often attends social functions and at last month's event he says to her, "Why aren't you more sociable at parties? You're so quiet. You must learn to enjoy yourself."

Then, at the following occasion, he says to her, "Please calm down. There's no need to be so noisy. You're becoming an embarrassment."

Manipulation and criticism are signs that there is not enough friendship bonding in the relationship. There is not enough openness, sharing, kindness and caring.

Controlling the environment

The need to constantly monitor and try to control the environment by training another's behaviour stems from a fear of the unfamiliar. If things are under your control the environment remains predictable and you are safe from potential pain within your own created structure.

Inserting another into your cage means that they are obliged to follow your rules. This unhealthy level of control leaves no room for creativity or wonderful surprises. When everything is dictated by a rulebook, the unexpected gifts of life that lie beyond the confines of the relationship cage will never be discovered.

Degrees of hurt

Why are some people easily hurt while other are seemingly unaffected by the opinions of others? This happens because everyone has different temperaments and varying needs for emotional validation. If someone gives another the responsibility for their emotional security, they are more likely to say they are hurt by the other's behaviour than those who do not give their emotional power away. During a relationship crisis some people actually do bleed to death emotionally; they do not have an efficient mechanism in place to enable them to stem the flow.

If your relationship with yourself is incomplete, there will always be opportunities to be hurt in relationship; it just depends on how long you choose to dwell on it or how personally you take it.

Unnecessary hurt and pain very often occur as a result of miscommunication and misunderstandings. When someone sees behaviour that reminds them of past deceit, they will be alerted because they have been conditioned to be wary of betrayal.

If you are in a relationship in which you feel hurt a lot of the time, you will have to ask yourself why you attracted a situation that would make you feel like this, and perhaps, even more importantly, why it is that you value affirmation from a person who is causing you pain. Is it possible that you are being oversensitive and overreacting to your partner's behaviour because of your own insecurities, and an inability to express your own needs and set your own boundaries? Are they triggering some of your own unresolved past hurt and pain?

Whose stuff is it?

We need to separate issues that emerge in relationship into *their stuff* and *my stuff*. You sometimes need to ask yourself how much of what you think is being said and done to you is actually your partner projecting their issues onto you. There has to be a clear line between what is really happening and what you think is happening. However, we always need to look at where we may have been wrong as well. It can sometimes be useful to reverse the hurtful situation and say, "Would I treat someone I love like this? If so, when, why and who would it be?"

When you are in harmony with yourself, there will be no need to inflict pain on others because it would be incongruent with how you are inside yourself and how you are in the world. However, if someone is filled with self-anger it can become so overwhelming that it spills out and contaminates the environment. A person in self-pain will look for the most efficient means of purging themselves of the intangible internal sensation. By releasing their venom onto another, the venom is given another life outside of themselves. The behaviour and responses of others give this pain a physical form and gives the sufferer – the source of the pain – some transient relief.

Those who do not like themselves will selectively dump their self-loathing onto people whom they intuitively know will accept it. If you feel as if people are using you as a garbage bin, stop wearing the label and keep the lid shut. Realise that the bin contains enough of your own stuff and that there is no space for anyone else's emotional garbage. It also does no-one any good to take on other people's stuff – it doesn't help them get rid of it – it just spreads and fills all the available space with toxic emotional waste; such is the nature of 'stuff'.

Moods

Although we may relate to ourselves and the world in a manner that is fairly consistent, we won't feel the same every day and won't always view things in the same light. Shifting and changing moods are a normal and expected part of being human – we are not robotic. We all have different responses to stimuli at different times, and they undulate along a fairly even plateau. However, if your mood swings are extreme, irrational, and cause you distress, they need to be addressed.

Are you depressed? You may find that you are taking on your partner's depression or vice-versa. When you suspect that you might be depressed, it is very important to look at possible organic causes of depression first. These could be: electrolyte imbalances, thyroid and hormone mal-functions, as well as other hormonal changes or deficiencies of certain minerals and/or vitamins. It is vital, therefore, to look at what we eat; the body does affect the mind.

Substance abuse also causes mood swings. In addition to the obvious non-prescription drugs like alcohol, cocaine and marijuana, substances that could affect your health and mood include: diet pills, steroids, cough remedies, flu medication, as well as certain prescription medications.

One also has to look at the genetic component of depression. What is your family history? Do you have an inherited tendency to developing a mood disorder? Also, growing up with a parent or parents with a mood disorder can be very threatening to a child and often these children suffer from anxiety and post traumatic stress disorder (PTSD). An unstable early environment can act as a trigger to 'switch on' the genetic potential to becoming depressed. Therefore, a child with the 'right' genes combined with a hostile environment is at a high risk of developing some form of mental pathology such as depression or PTSD.

The Zung Self-Rating Depression Scale is a useful screening tool in which a 20-item self-report questionnaire is used to assess an individual for the affective (mood disturbance), psychological (depression and/or anxiety) and somatic symptoms (fibromyalgia, chronic fatigue and pain) associated with depression. Select the options that you feel are most appropriate and add up the scores for each item to get your total. Most people suffering from depression score between 50 and 69 points on this scale. If your score is 70 and higher, it indicates severe depression. Note: The Zung questionnaire is a useful tool in assessing possible depression; it is NOT a substitute for an interview with a health practitioner.

	A little of the time	Some of the time	Good part of the time	Most of the time
1. I feel down-hearted and blue	1	2	3	4
2. Morning is when I feel the best	4	3	2	1
3. I have crying spells or feel like it	1	2	3	4
4. I have trouble sleeping at night	1	2	3	4
5. I eat as much as I used to	4	3	2	1
6. I still enjoy sex	4	3	2	1
7. I notice that I am losing weight	1	2	3	4
8. I have trouble with constipation	1	2	3	4
9. My heart beats faster than usual	1	2	3	4
10. I get tired for no reason	1	2	3	4
11. My mind is as clear as it used to be	4	3	2	1
12. I find it easy to do the things I used to	4	3	2	1
13. I am restless and can't keep still	1	2	3	4
14. I feel hopeful about the future	4	3	2	1
15. I am more irritable than usual	1	2	3	4
16. I find it easy to make decisions	4	3	2	1
17. I feel that I am useful and needed	4	3	2	1
18. My life is pretty full	4	3	2	1
19. I feel that others would be better off if I were dead	1	2	3	4
20. I still enjoy the things I used to do	4	3	2	1

How do you feel about your moods?

How do you relate to your own mood changes? Maybe there are different personalities that emerge under different circumstances. Why is that? Maybe it's because a certain situation or a word reminds you of a time in the past, and you become who you were then?

When a mood comes in, try to welcome it. Give it form and sit with it.

- When have you met this mood before?
- What were the circumstances?
- Was the mood in response to a fear of loss or perhaps an uncomfortable feeling that you were not able to define or place?
- Was the mood associated with emotional pain?
- How did it play out for you on the previous occasion?
- What issue, word or action invited this mood in today?
- What are your levels of self-worth at the moment?

Breaking the cycle

The Catch-22 of a negative mood is that when you are experiencing a down frame of mind, the only other images you are able to see will be framed in the same way. Your mind will flash images of all the bad and dark things that have happened to you in the past and your pessimism will increase. It is extremely important for you to find ways to break this cycle. Make an effort to think happy thoughts and to smile! Smiling fools your brain into thinking that you are happy.

Find a picture that is uplifting and peaceful and copy it into your mind. Choose rather to go there – to the imagined happy place – than to get stuck in negative thoughts. Movement to music is another wonderful way to create joyful spaces. Once you can find the up feeling again, you will access all your sunny, optimistic memories and you will feel hope returning to your space.

Detached mood

Sometimes a detached mood can be triggered when a person is in desperate need of a safe place. Although they are physically with you, it may seem as if they are no longer present; their personality has been abducted. This person has learned this type of protective behaviour in an attempt to escape childhood hostility and you may find that they created secret places for themselves, places in which to hide in order to feel safe. When a relationship becomes threatening because something is reminding them of a past experience, they 'wink out.' They are physically present but absent on all other levels. This is not conscious – it is an old, learned method of self-preservation.

If you find that this happens to you, try to isolate the incident that triggers your fear response. It will, more than likely, be a circumstance that you perceive as one of abandonment or rejection; a situation in which you feel disempowered because it reminds you of how disempowered you felt as a child. Your thoughts return to those times and now, as an adult, you forget that you can express your wishes and opinions without fear of punishment.

Fear

Changes occur in our bodies and our minds when we are confronted with a fearful situation. This happens regardless of whether the threat is real or imagined. Stress is good when you need the energy to run away from a life-threatening situation, but it is bad when you are sitting in an office chair trying to escape an unwanted phone call.

In other words, you can think yourself scared and your body will release adrenalin, cortisol and noradrenalin to gear you up for a quick escape. Your physiology cannot tell the difference between what is real and what is imagined, and your instinctive response is survival. During a flight or fight response, your heart rate and blood pressure increase and you prepare yourself to face or escape the danger. But what if there is no actual threat and you remain sitting in your adrenalised soup? You will become anxious – because you live in fear of what you have decided might happen – and your body tells your mind that it is ready to race; your mind remembers a fearful situation.

A useful technique to turn to in these circumstances is an ancient yoga exercise called *The Complete Breath*. For this exercise, use your entire respiratory system. Breathe through your nostrils and fill your lungs with air while focusing your attention on your breath and on your body. Take a deep breath, hold it for a few seconds, and then exhale slowly. Repeat this with conscious intent for a few minutes until you feel more relaxed.

Secrets

Keeping secrets from your partner can cause you a great deal of unnecessary stress and anxiety. Making decisions for your future or organising important events in your personal life without consulting or including your partner puts your relationship under heavy pressure. If you are living a secret life outside of your relationship, you may need to question why you are still in a committed relationship with your partner. Also, what is preventing you from being honest?

Allergies

Allergies can also cause mood changes. Is the fabric you wear affecting how you feel in your skin; or is the food you eat making you uncomfortable? Sometimes there are also circumstances and situations that leave us feeling irritable and tired. On an emotional level, you can ask yourself: "To what am I allergic? Which people or situations in my life do I have an aversion to right now? Is it possible I'm feeling emotionally congested or blocked?"

Arguments – fighting for happiness?

The most interesting oxymoron of our time has to be *peace-keeping force*. It is as futile to send troops into a foreign country to force a coalition government as it is to fight with one another to create a better relationship. War is used to gain control because control creates a perceived sense of safety in uncharted territories – this is especially true in the unexplored arena of a relationship. Do you find yourself constantly trying to establish your territorial advantage?

The history of the world is filled with eras of conflict and invasions and men going off to war. Today, life has become easier in that sense so we have resorted to engaging in sport-war. All the adrenalin that was used in the past to go into battle is now used to shout for (or play for) our chosen team – either seen on the television or live at the sports grounds. We align ourselves with specific teams and the supporters of the opposition team become the enemy. This is how many of us wage vicarious wars these days. And partners can even have fights over the sport-war because one partner does not like to spend the day watching it whereas the other does.

Debatable negotiation

There is a difference between engaging in a constructive conversation or debate and having an emotional argument. It would be unnatural to share your life, your space, and your heart with another and not have disagreements. The key is whether the relationship is strengthened or weakened by this, and whether your differing opinions can be reconciled. Often arguments start because we jump to conclusions; we incorrectly frame circumstances in our personal paradigm of past experiences. A useful way to avoid unnecessary arguments is to take a breath and count to ten before assuming anything. We need to be objective and consciously look at what is really happening.

During an emotionally charged argument, it is unlikely that either of you is listening to the other. You are both knee-jerking and too busy unpacking your stock responses to respond to what's happening in the now. Both of you are determined to put up barriers in self-defense; either proactively or reactively. You want to win the war and neither partner is interested in negotiating.

These skirmishes are usually triggered by some sort of behaviour by one party that creates an uncomfortable feeling in the other. The emotional discomfort then causes this person to respond. People usually respond negatively if they either consider that someone else's behaviour is meant to make them feel inadequate in some way, or if it directly threatens their sense of self-worth. Your self-worth, however, can be put at risk only if most of your identity is invested in the behaviour of another. By actively surrendering your power within a relationship, you assume a position of disempowerment by default.

If you over-invest in another, you tend to neglect investing in yourself. Your personal growth and your wellbeing are sacrificed in favour of fulfilling another's needs because you have chosen to make your partner your life's purpose. Ultimately, your partner's life becomes your obsession

– at your expense – and you end up losing your identity because he or she defines you.

"I am not worthy as I am. I only have my self-worth if you give it to me because I am an extension of you. And now you have taken it away by making me feel like this. For this reason, I will become defensive because I feel vulnerable. I hold you responsible for my emotional stability."

But the truth is seldom verbalised like this; often because it is not actually recognised. Our arguments usually start with, "Why do we always do what you want to do? I do everything for you. I gave up my life to be with you and make you happy. Look what I get in return."

Is it jealousy?

If your response-behaviour is caused by jealousy, it could be that you have feelings of insecurity and you need the undivided attention of your partner to feel safe and validated. If you see that your partner can be entertained by anything (a person or a hobby) other than you, you will feel threatened. It is very important in these instances that you spend time working on your relationship with yourself. Feeling comfortable and liking who you are will stop you entertaining thoughts of unworthiness. This in turn will help diminish your fear of losing your relationship with your partner.

Comparing yourself with others is self-destructive and futile. Unfortunately, we are enculturated into a society that supports hierarchies of comparison. We are often asked about our marital status, our qualifications, how much we earn, the car we drive, where we live, and so on. There will always be people who are better off and worse off than ourselves; better looking and worse looking; luckier and unluckier than us. This gives us plenty of material to work with, if we so choose. Comparison with others is an endless waste of energy and it is up to you to stop competing with others and focus on being yourself.

However, if your partner is selfish and ignores you when you are out socialising, or if your partner has a constant need to flirt, do not waste your time and energy fighting about it. This is how they are in their relationship with you. They have a need to be seen (sometimes they like to be viewed as available) and a need for attention. You have the option of making them fully available to everyone by ending your relationship. Alternatively, you could use this opportunity to grow in self-respect. If you change your attitude towards yourself, your relationship *will* change. If you want to be respected, you need to respect yourself. Once you have learned the lesson that this relationship brought you, you can decide whether to stay or go.

A half truth is still a whole lie

Unfortunately, our rationale does become fudged with perceived threats during emotional outbursts, and our visceral response to these perceived threats is to default to old patterns of protection that we learned through past experiences. These kinds of responses occur because we remember past events – especially those times in which vital emotional information was withheld from us. Your partner may have been doing any number of things behind your back; and when you found out, it caused you a lot of heartache because you felt betrayed.

You may, in later times, see clues that trigger the memory of how you were deceived, and you will think, "This is happening again. This time I'm not going to be lied to." When you first get a sniff of something, try to gather all the information from the best source as soon as possible. Having access to only half of a picture is problematic because the rest is left up to your imagination. And after all, a half truth is still a whole lie.

Do not get involved in speculation – speculation leads nowhere and is a waste of time and energy, not to mention the fact that it's counter-productive. The scenarios floating around in your head are likely to stimulate an emotional response – a response based on something that may not even be true.

Having had a past experience of being deceived will obviously make you more wary because you do not want to be bitten again. However, be very sure that your current response is realistic and not based on past programming before you launch a counter-attack.

Feeling and meaning

Some people are programmed to find intensity and feeling through having an argument. Relationships with these people typically end up as 'hire-and-fire' relationships. The bonds of attachment are built around making up and breaking up because a stable relationship without the fighting is too boring. The action-arguments spice up the environment and add flavour to the anticipation of the making-up ritual.

The reality is that arguments rarely have a positive outcome because they end up dividing the partners into two separate camps – and this scenario rapidly devolves into a power struggle. Communication then degenerates into conflict; our togetherness is replaced by a *me-versus-you* attitude. Instead of honouring differences we are creating division.

Projection

When you point fingers and ask: "Do you really love me?" or "What did you do last night?" are you asking yourself or your partner? There is often a tendency to act out one's own guilt as if it were that of the other. You need reassurance that that they are not doing or thinking what you are doing or thinking because you know how easy it is to deceive. But why are you deceiving?

Sometimes, our partners may start an argument to get a response from us when they are feeling insecure. This often happens when they feel that they are not getting the sort of attention that they have become accustomed to, or should be getting. Maybe you have changed your outlook and behaviour and this is unsettling for your partner. In order to re-establish his zone of safety, he will start prodding away to see what you do. "Do I still have the same effect on her? Am I still important?" This is a pre-linguistic way of dealing with issues. As adults, we need to understand that we can communicate our issues of insecurity to our partners. We can talk now. Throwing the toys around will not achieve the same outcome as it did when we were still children.

Here are some common problems in relationships that may lead to unnecessary arguments:

- **"My partner does not understand how I feel."** Do you tell your partner how you feel; or do you assume that they should just know? Are you unable to discuss your feelings with your partner? If so, why not? It is important to assess how much communication is happening in your relationship – not only about the relationship, but about general issues both trivial and profound. Do you share thoughts and ideas with one another? Do you laugh together? There is a profoundly simple saying that sums up the communication in a relationship – "*Those who pray together stay together.*" This need have nothing to do with religion and everything to do with the opening of the heart in a fundamental way.

- **Sex.** If the relationship is good, this forms 5% of the partnership. It is the act that seals all that is good between you. If the relationship is problematic, 95% of the focus of arguments will be about sex, in one way or the other. Some factors contributing towards not feeling sexually attractive are: stress and fatigue, a demanding job, and feeling rejected by your partner. The rejection feeling can occur as a result of seeing your partner flirting continuously with others which makes you feel less physically attractive to him or her; or one of the partners may have had an affair, which leaves the other feeling resentful because the underlying cause was never dealt with and the symptom was pacified; or perhaps the other partner has withdrawn without any reasonable explanation. Some people believe that sex is the only way to demonstrate affection. Over a period of time, we should be able to move away from the emphasis on the physical and rediscover other dimensions and facets within our relationships, our partners, and ourselves.

- **"We argue about everything."** You cannot argue with an open heart, so this type of response is an indication of underlying fears. What are they? Why do you need to be defensive and competitive? Why do you have an unhealthy need to always be right? And what exactly have you won when you win an argument? This unbearable rightness-of-being has a profound effect on everything around it. A person who has this need to always be right usually has a fear of losing control (power), and will use anger to stop others from asserting themselves. They often have rigid belief patterns and insist on getting their way.

This is a fear-based stance in which the individual does not want to be seen as vulnerable and they often perceive themselves as being criticised by others. Ironically, although they act superior, they usually have a great need for the approval of others. This concept of 'my way or the highway' spreads through couples, families, societies, and even through nations. Throughout history we have witnessed both wars and slavery resulting from this narrow-minded need to be right. We should all learn to say, "I don't know everything," and "Sorry, I was wrong."

- **"He does little things that really irritate me."** When did these personal ways start to irritate you? In this situation it could be useful to look at anger you may be carrying because of bigger things that are happening, or have happened, that you are not addressing. For example, if he drinks too much every night, you may lose respect for him and then start finding him generally unattractive. You will start picking around the issue instead of addressing the root cause – the drinking, and why he feels a need to drink now.

- **"This relationship was never the same after we had children."** Choosing to be a parent means that you will need to reinvent yourself. When you and your partner met you were buddies, then lovers, and then committed – most likely in a relationship bound by the conforms of marriage. You became husband and wife but your focus was still on one another. You were nurturing the 'relationship-child' that you birthed together. Once you had children, you became father and mother to that human child, and the focus was no longer on each other – or on your relationship. All your energy and conversation revolved around your offspring. And now? Is this all you have in common; are you living your life through your children?

- **Mid-life crisis.** This is a time when people act out all the things they always wanted to do but never felt they could. It is not something new or out of character. It is what they would have done had they not had other responsibilities or had they not given up who they were in the relationship. Often people grow apart within a relationship because they settle for what they are getting out of it in other ways. The relationship may provide them with financial security, or status, or it may be a means to having some other ambition fulfilled. It's nice to have the person there because they have become a means to an end. People grow apart because they forget to share the important events like a sunset or the moon rise or a new flower opening. They are always together at the unimportant social occasions though. Over the years, the separation creeps in and you suddenly realise that you never talk and have not done so for ages. This mid-life opportunity gives you the space to experiment and grow. This is a time when it's best to use all the information and lessons from the past and start applying them productively. Alternatively, you can regress to being an adolescent. It is your choice.

• **The Glue-Pot.** Men do seem to be more guilty of this than women. This is the place where they get stuck on their way back home. Sometimes they get a call from the glue-pot – a friend or a buddy – for just one drink. Arguments arise because she is told to look after the kids while he goes out; she doesn't like sitting in the glue pot; she doesn't like how he is when he returns from it; he doesn't like being criticised so he stays at the glue pot. It is a warm fuzzy zone in which bonding outside of the real world takes place – at the expense of their primary relationship.

One must always bear in mind that a situation can only be resolved at the level at which it was created. So it can be useful to look at your relationship foundation and see when and where the problem was inserted. Everything built on top of an unaddressed issue will be unstable and will therefore create more of the same issues. It's never advisable to build on a fault line.

The structuring of arguments

What is typically your response in an argument? Do you take it personally? Was it really a personal attack? Do you feel as if your self-worth is being sabotaged because you depend on the approval of the other?

Some people find it impossible not to reflect back to the person in an argument. The knee-jerk response to anything will be, "But *you* ..." Past events are used as weapons and ammunition is gathered, over time, to fill the artillery. Why do you not look at the behaviour and the current situation objectively, and play the ball – not the person? What is it that you feel that you need to protect? Are you breaking them down because your fear of losing them is so great? Is that logical? What about the fear of seeming weak? And what about the idiotic response of, "I understand," which does nothing to resolve the situation.

Sometimes one can get stuck in a habit of arguing in circles. This translates into fixing the same mistakes with the same glue – and you stay stuck together with the same problems as a result.

- Why are you arguing?
- Look at the situation as if it were happening to someone else.
- What do you hope to achieve?
- Is this situation solvable?
- How does provocation serve your emotional needs?
- Do you want this relationship to end, but don't have the strength of character to take on the responsibility of that decision?

Have you ever tried to hold hands while arguing? Generally during conflict, we recoil from making non-aggressive physical contact with the 'enemy' because it feels like a violation of our personal space. Making gentle unobtrusive contact will enable you to open your hearts more to one another, but both parties must want a resolution.

Communication habits

The first question one must ask is, "How were you trained to communicate as a child?" And secondly, "What was the level of hostility and tension in your childhood environment?" Were you encouraged to express and defend yourself freely, or were you silenced into submission?

If you were raised in a household in which you interpreted too much calm as dangerous, you will interpret calm as unfamiliar and unpredictable. For you, it really was the lull before the storm. If you received this kind of conditioning, it will feel safer creating chaos than waiting for the chaos to attack you. The peace and quiet will create tension within you that needs to be released. This type of training produces a person who will not believe in the permanence of something good; you will end up creating a life of self-fulfilling prophecies by destroying any potential of lasting peace through your constant need for crises; you cannot trust the stillness because you believe that it is followed by hostility and violence.

The words that will be stored are, "My house; my rules." In other words, your safety as a child was threatened if you spoke up for yourself because 'house' meant food and shelter to you – without which you thought you would die. Later on in life, this type of training can create intense anxiety when you are asked for your opinion, because you are put into a perceived double-bind situation. You want to express your opinion, but do not know if you will survive if you do – yet if you do not say anything, you will retreat, boiling with resentment.

Were you told to "go to your room and be quiet" when you expressed an opinion or defended yourself? If so, you will have learned that disputes could not be resolved through communication. You were never heard and you will therefore understand that sitting alone in your room is the way problems are resolved; your programming is that you do not engage with anyone on any level because your opinion will neither be heard nor affirmed. Conflict resolution is achieved through silence and isolation.

Defending yourself and/or your position could also have been incorrectly programmed if you were punished for standing up for yourself and for telling the truth. If you returned home after school after being beaten up by a classmate and your mother said, "It must have been your fault. What did you do to make him hit you?" you would have learned that defending yourself is futile because you don't get the support or the empathy you need from your caregiver. You learn that whatever happens to you is your fault; that the other person is innocent and you feel punished for their behaviour and are rejected for being honest. Later on in life, you may take on unrealistic responsibility for issues that have nothing to do with you because somehow you will feel that you are to blame; you are the cause of the problem. You may also find that you avoid discussing issues in which you feel you may be judged or reprimanded. So when your partner or someone else asks, "What's wrong? What happened?" you might instinctively say, "Nothing."

All these learned behaviours are carried into adulthood. So, if a vulnerable memory button is pressed, you as an adult will process the situation as a child again; reflexing back to past behaviour but now acting in the adult paradigm. We can put up invisible walls, sit alone in a room, disappear into the computer, or get lost in a book or in music. Anything that allows us to detach from a situation that is perceived as uncomfortable and unsafe; we will default to the imprint that worked best for us in the past. We will choose the means to dissipate the anger, anxiety and feelings of unworthiness of being dismissed and invisible. Up until now, it is the only way we knew how. However, if we make a change and start thinking things through, we can transform our old patterned way of responding and create new and realistic outcomes and a healthier self respect.

Chatting without goals

Sometimes we just want to shoot the breeze, to flesh something out, and we do not necessarily want solutions. Having a discussion with someone often helps us to define and formulate our own solutions by being given the opportunity gain objectivity through verbalising a situation. It is much easier to gain clarity when speaking aloud to someone than it is when you mull it over in your own head.

It is very useful to be in the company of those who facilitate your process by listening, rather than those who immediately say, "That's easy. Why don't you just do this or that? Why do you have to talk about it, just sort it out." How lovely it is to be in the company of someone who realises that humans have two ears and one mouth, and who uses them in that ratio, listening twice as much as they speak. There is a difference between quick-fixing and creatively maintaining.

Really hearing and acknowledging another person means taking our own position and subjectivity out of the equation. Most people listen with their own circumstance top of mind. As they hear the words of another, their mind is saying, "How does this affect me? How can I relate myself to this circumstance? Where do I fit in here? What about me?"

Ideally they should turn down the volume of their inner chatter so that they can truly hear the other, and have the space in which to receive the message of the other.

Realistically, the other person is relaying a situation that is not about you. It is not your experience. It is about them. It is their stuff. It is useful to perceive the difference between your issues and someone else's, and not to get the boundaries tangled up. Their circumstance is as different from yours as you are as individuals, but their story will intersect (if you allow this) at the point at which it provokes your safety zone. So, if your partner's issues make you feel abandoned, that is your problem – not theirs. Because of this, you may try to insert yourself into their situation so that you, too, belong in their process; so that you feel part of their issue. You need to be part of their dynamics otherwise you feel left out because so much of yourself is entangled with them, and you've inserted so much of them into yourself. You identify so fully with them that you think you are safe within their problems.

If one person struggles with the concept of change, they will not cope with the other making changes in their life because their sense of order and control will be disrupted. Interestingly, it is these inflexible people with inefficient listening skills who are often the ones to say, "I had no idea!" when the relationship ends (or the quiet guy next door turns out to be a serial killer).

"This comes as such a shock! Why didn't you tell me there was a problem?" he says.

Why didn't you listen?

Other clues

Metacommunication, or non-verbal communication, can give us very interesting clues about what is really happening within our relationship.

Look to your own and to other people's body language. The connection between mind and body, and body and mind, is so intimately intertwined that our thoughts are demonstrated in our bodies. Look at how your partner positions him or herself near you. Does she cross her legs away from you or towards you? Are there signs that you are being excluded from conversations by lack of eye contact? Or that invisible electromagnetic feeling of being repelled when he walks past you – like two north poles of a magnet. Evidence of detached avoidance usually means there is a problem.

Words

Linguistic cues are also relevant. Look at their choice of words and how they phrase what is being said. Are there more *I*'s than *we*'s lately? How are words used? If someone is defaulting to, "I am going away this weekend" or "I am inviting some people over for supper," it is an indication that this person is dissociating from their relationship. They think of themselves as single.

Health

Health can also be a very good indicator of what is happening underneath the veneer, in the unspoken space. If your partner often has a sore throat, they are very likely withholding themselves from expressing what is troubling them. A cough or chest infection indicates that there is a problem around feeling vulnerable within the relationship. The expression of their heart is feeling damaged and tired.

Sulking

Sulking is probably the most obvious – and the most useless – form of metacommunication. It is self-indulgent behaviour that is counter-productive and selfish. Somewhere a sulker has learned to puff up as an attention-seeking strategy because it worked for them somewhere. Somehow the sulker gets a pay-off from this behaviour; the emotion feels good. It has become a form of protection and a means of creating a safe space, because they learn to manipulate others to pacify their own insecurities and need for attention. It is fear-related behaviour, and the sulker has to learn that there are better and quicker ways of getting the emotional security that they need as an adult. It may have worked for them as children, but the behaviour is redundant in adulthood. We grow up and have the necessary vocabulary to voice our fears and not to retreat in self-pity with a closed heart. One cannot reach any solution through sulking. Staying in an environment contaminated by a sulker is a waste of time.

Open and honest communication

Open and honest communication is probably the most important element in a healthy relationship. As soon as there are fuzzy zones, the door to speculation is opened. If someone is being deceitful, it will show in their behaviour, and the person with whom they are in a relationship will detect their lack of honesty and act on it. The usual response will be to take it as a personal insult because he or she feels that their partner is not sharing openly. The assumption is 'something is happening behind my back' and this leads to mistrust and emotionally defensive behaviour by the other. Very often, innocent situations are blown way out of proportion purely because simple and often harmless information is being withheld. Have the courage to speak your truth – it always comes out in the end anyway. But bear in mind that you can only speak your truth if you are honest with yourself to begin with.

What do you do to express how you feel? Do you withhold your emotions out of fear – and if so, what is it that you fear? Does the scary monster in your head inhibit you from expressing what you really mean?

Often when people feel compromised in fully expressing themselves, they do it in roundabout ways. It is like dancing with an agenda, and the agenda is provocative. You take two steps forward and I'll take two steps back – "If you are good to me, I'll be good to you." It becomes a game of subliminal ping-pong. "I'll give in if you give in; I'll say I love you when you say it." Your relationship becomes a conditional game, because you feel that you are somehow being compromised.

Ideally, both of you should take a break from all the subterfuge, and be mature enough to sit down and speak the unspoken words.

Be congruent in all your relationships. Love your friends and love your partner. It is illogical to be able to show your pet love and to not have the willingness do the same for your partner. Do you find it easier to act lovingly towards animals than towards the people in your life? If so, why is that? What is it about loving a human that makes you feel unsafe? It is true that animals teach us purity of spirit and unconditional love.

Possibly, your message to the other is how you wish to be treated; rather as a companion animal than a whipping boy.

Our lesson of learning to love others and ourselves unconditionally is one of the greatest and most difficult, but it does come with the highest reward. If you love without needing to be loved in return – but simply to share your heart because that is how you are – love will always be returned.

Do not martyr and sabotage yourself by loving someone who has no feelings for you or for themselves. This is pathological and self-destructive and is usually an attempt to recover or make right a past relationship (often parental). If you are drawn to people who are detached and emotionally absent, why is it that you look for affirmation from this type of person?

Remember that love is not just a noun, it's also a verb. So do it.

Blaming

Sadly, we have become a society of victims. It is always someone else's fault. Why do we need to blame others? "You just tell me what to do all the time." Is that a statement or an instruction?

You cannot blame someone else if they do what you have told them to do. Did you choose to be with someone because you need external rules and structure? Are you really able to take responsibility for your decisions or do you find it easier to blame others than to stand by your own choices?

"It's because of you that I don't have a life; I gave up everything for you. It's not fair." Is it realistic to give someone else so much power over you? What was the pay-off for you when you decided to martyr yourself for this person and this relationship? There must have been some agenda – was it your desire to have children, a lifestyle, status, or your fear of living alone?

The beginning of blame

What were the rules in your parents' home? If you took instruction from an authoritarian figure during your childhood, it is highly likely that you will continue to do so in your adult relationships. If you were raised in an environment in which you had to follow the instructions of a parent without being allowed to question the rationale, you have been programmed to wait for directives. You need pointers; some indication of where to go and what to do next. And as you listen and carry out orders you will learn to think, "But you told me to do it," and "It's not my fault, it wasn't me. It wasn't my decision."

This happens as a result of not expressing your own opinion during your formative years and not knowing what it feels like to make a choice or a decision for yourself. All your decisions were made for you and your opinion was irrelevant. You had no voice. This is how you learned to gain acceptance – through conditional behaviour. "If you listen to me you can stay. You're under my roof now and you'll follow my rules." A double-bind situation may also occur if the child is instructed to accept the consequences of his or her actions, and is then told to follow instructions without question. The child is then punished for something he or she was told to do – the classic damned-if-you-do, damned-if-you-don't scenario. This causes great difficulty later on in life because these people never know what they want – they do not feel they have the right to have wants, and they have never been trained to find their own direction. They were trained to fit in and follow the herd because that is how it's always been done.

Not surprisingly, when the child returns home with a problem and says, "I don't know what to do with my life. Tell me." The parent says, "It's your choice. I'm seriously not going to be responsible for your decisions." How do parents expect children to make informed decisions as adults if they were never affirmed in this regard during their growing years?

Because you never saw the possibility of expressing your ideals and ideas, you forget how to have them. In later years, you will come to depend on others giving you instructions. And when they do, you will blame them because you still resent not being recognised for who you are and how you feel. But do you know who you are? Do you borrow opinions from others because of a need for acceptance, or a desire to pacify a situation? How deeply do you fear being rejected or punished for expressing your opinion?

The passive-aggressive behaviour of wanting instructions and then blaming the instructor is a futile cycle. Although your need for acceptance is being fulfilled, your need for self-expression is being smothered.

So, when you cannot breathe, you blame another for your feelings of loss of self.

"What do you want?" they ask you.

"I don't know. What do you want?" you answer.

You delegate the responsibility of your choices to someone else because you are too scared to say what you want to for fear of rejection and maybe loss. They make the decisions for you because you asked them to do so, but when they do, you say, "It's your fault. I would never have done this if it were not for you. It's not fair. You always make all the decisions for me. Do you ever consider what it is that I may want? What about me?"

When are we going to step out of our victim thinking – blaming past people for our current circumstances? We're feeling, thinking beings who can step outside of situations and assess them for what they really are. And we have the free will to make different choices.

Take charge of your life

What about you? What do you want? Find out what you want, and take responsibility for your choices; or remain an extension of someone else's decision-making process. If you don't decide for yourself, someone else will. Do you come from a community or a family that is constantly blaming some outside influence for their dilemma? Blaming external forces is essentially saying, "I can't do this because I am incapable of expressing my will." You keep saying everything is their fault – and yet you expect them to direct you.

You are *where* you are because of *who* you are and the degree to which you are willing to be responsible and accountable for your actions. Blaming is victim mentality. Why do you choose to be a victim? Victims survive on self-pity and the only way out is to stop feeling sorry for yourself; to reclaim your personal power. You gave it away; now take it back. You cannot honestly expect someone else to give your dignity back to you? Why do they have it in the first place?

Your disempowerment came about solely through your choice to surrender it to someone else. To whom do you now surrender your personal power?

WINNERS, LOSERS, AND FREE SPIRITS

I bring to you the message of unity and understanding ... to appreciate the value of the gifts you receive by sharing with one another.

Entering into a relationship means that you have chosen a particular person with whom to form a partnership. Combining both your strengths will therefore ideally create a far better outcome than each of you putting all your energy into a power struggle. If one partner is inflexible and the other is unstructured, don't let the differences divide you – join the poles and find a compromise. Look for the middle ground and for the learning opportunities in that zone of possibilities.

Competition

By its very nature, competition is hostile – to win the competition you need to treat your partner as an opponent, someone to whom you are opposed.

Competition generally involves a race to grab resources that are perceived as scarce. As a child, your primary needs were love, shelter and food. Maybe that is where you started believing that things could be finite. Maybe you did not get nurturing when you needed it, which unfortunately resulted in your being incorrectly programmed.

When, as children, we are trained to receive *conditional* positive regard, this creates irrational behaviour within us as adults. If we do find someone to nurture us, we do not believe it can last because we still expect it to be withdrawn from us at an unpredictable moment. As adults, we continue to react with the mistrust we developed as children.

As a child, this was rational behaviour because you were dependent on your primary caregiver for survival. Now, as an independent adult, it is irrational to insert your vulnerable child-memories into your current adult interactions in the hope of receiving emotional acknowledgement. You need to realise that you no longer need to work for acceptance and survival, and that the person with whom you are now in a relationship is not your parent, but your partner and equal.

Do you compete with one another for affirmation within a relationship? Competition between partners in a relationship is the same as playing power games. Your aim is to get points. You did this, therefore there is one point against you; I did that so I have one point in my favour. It becomes a debit and credit system. "The more things you do wrong, the more I make you feel indebted to me and I will remind you that you owe me."

Some people prefer the other to be in the 'wrong' most of the time so that they, themselves, can always feel victimised. They have something to complain about to their friends and those who will listen, so they can receive sympathy such as, "Shame, she has such a hard life with him." Often this is not a conscious choice – she has learned the 'victim habit', which somehow makes her feel that she has control.

Sometimes people compete against their partner's previous relationships. "See how much better I am than your ex." Or they compete with a potential future relationship, "You'll never find someone as good as me again."

Unfortunately, competition within any partnership – whether it be friendship or other – can only result in your feeling isolated because the relationship is set up in such a way that you are opposing teams. You are fighting to stay in a partnership, instead of sharing.

Why are we attracted to people with whom we wish to compete? Are we looking for the weakness in another to show our own strength? Do you engage in intellectual sparring matches to say to someone, "See how clever I actually am?" Why do you need to prove your worth through this person's acknowledgement of you? Maybe you are still trying to reconcile unfulfilled parental recognition?

Once a relationship becomes a dual its essence will be based on who is maintaining the upper hand. But, who is actually winning? You think you are surviving because you are proving your worthiness; but this entire act is useless and worthless because it proves nothing except that you are insecure.

Constant competitiveness can have one of two outcomes. Firstly, you can successfully drive the other away, or secondly, you can drive the other to become more competitive, and – depending on their personality – to be more spiteful and vengeful. Competition is innately hostile, no matter how we try to disguise it and call it healthy. There is always a loser who is vanquished by the winner.

Prodding the green monster

Reasonable or realistic jealousy in a relationship is normal; pathological jealousy is not. It is useful to know the difference. If jealousy is becoming the overriding emotion, you need to deal with your own issues relating to insecurity or inferiority – or look at why you are being made to feel this way so often in this relationship. Does your partner need to make you jealous to pacify their own insecurities? Do you find them saying, "I was invited out tonight by someone who is quite interesting, but I decided not to go." Or maybe, "He said I should call him as soon as I'm single again."

Jealousy usually occurs when one partner feels that someone else is getting what he or she is lacking *most* from their chosen relationship partner. If you are in a relationship with someone who does not communicate well with you and you hear them having a long chat on the phone with someone else, this will make you feel envious. You will think, "Why can he talk to her like that and not to me?" Or, if you feel that you are lacking affection from your partner and you see him or her acting affectionately towards others, this will amplify your feelings of emotional deprivation. You will realise that she has the capacity to be affectionate, just not with you. If your partner never spends money on you – either buying you a meal or small gifts – but does so for others, you will feel short-changed.

Ideally, people should be congruent across all their relationships and not resort to putting on masks to suit different occasions. Sometimes people appear to have a confused self image – they behave differently with different people or in different circumstances. If your partner is mostly more alive and happy in the company of others, you will have to question why he or she cannot be the same when they are alone with you. How many personalities does this person have?

You may be feeling that you have not been getting the kind of attention that you need in order to feel safe and special in your relationship. The worst thing to do would be to try to compete with another person whom you believe is taking the attention away from you. You are different and have other admirable qualities. Do not focus on the person who makes you feel jealous. The more attention you give to this person, the more life you breathe into them and, ironically, you will be the one inserting them into your relationship and into your life. Your preoccupation with that 'other person' gives them entry into your space. Let the thought of them go.

The trophy

Ideally, a relationship is meant to be a joint venture. In other words, you work together towards a common goal and you share what you have. Don't try to outdo your partner. Rather choose to support their strengths. A relationship is not a bullfight between a bull and a matador where you show off your clever tactics to one another. This is not how you win affection; and at a very basic level you are actually just trying to impress them by saying, "I beat you at your own game. Please admire me now." In other words, you have set them as your gold standard – otherwise there would be no need to compete with them. You want them to fully identify with your potential and your ability – and for this reason you set about trying to conquer them by plundering their worthiness.

Is this the trophy that you really want? Does it justify the effort? Is the outcome worth it? Will they really think you are a better person once you've damaged them by beating them? Will they admire you more? How can you break someone's spirit and claim that you love them?

Girl power?

Women create their own problems by competing with one other on both overt and covert levels. Men generally compete overtly and mostly bond to anaesthetise themselves against their emotions; to share some reality-avoidance time. Women often get together because they want to flesh out their emotions to understand why their relationships are playing out as they are. Using problems as the topic of conversation and a means of getting attention becomes tedious unless the focus is solution-driven. The more we dwell on what is wrong in our lives, the more energy we invest in it and the more problems we create. If we could all make an effort to spend less of our free time giving valuable attention to negative issues and actively looking for positives instead, we would all be a lot more optimistic and productive.

But where is the real support between women? Does the need to dress up to compete really exist? Do women flirt with unavailable men because they can see he has the ability to commit; at the same time trying to turn him into something else by initiating an affair? Do you fear love? Is that why you choose someone unavailable? Or is it simply that you need to compete with his or her current partner to win his affection and so prove your attractiveness or self-worth? The relevant question could be, "Did you perhaps compete with one parent for the other parent's affection?"

Another question one needs to ask is, "Why do women squeeze themselves into other women's marriages by having affairs with a married man?" This means that the problems in his marriage are never addressed since he is finding a distraction elsewhere and is living with guilt at home. You are the dummy that is pacifying his unhappy marriage.

Who are your friends when you are single and happy or when you are single and unhappy?

Who are your friends after a divorce or a separation? Often, after a break-up or a divorce, your 'couple' friends suddenly alienate themselves from you and choose to form an alliance with your ex-partner. One should not need to compete for friends or support during times of stress.

Coalitions based on negative experiences never bode well for the future. There are those who bond to forget the bad, and those who bond to dwell on it.

What happens when you start a new relationship? Do you have friends who try to compete with you for the attention of your new partner? No true friend would try to insert themselves into your relationship in any manner.

Sometimes we have friends who are used to us being single and available for them at all times, and when we become involved in a relationship, our new partner is seen as a threat. Our friends may start competing with our partners for our time and attention because we are not as accessible to them as we were in the past.

$$1+1 = 3 \quad : \quad 1-1 = 0$$

Try out new and different ways of doing things and explore your own potential instead of staying stuck in *my way or the highway*. Remember that one plus one does equal three, and one minus one equals zero. Stop competing with one another; do what you do best and love your partner as yourself. That is more than enough. It's really quite simple: synergy or destruction. Which do you want?

Betrayal

Betrayal implies that someone is lying and people generally lie because they do not feel safe telling the truth. Feelings of betrayal and hurt are deepest when two people make a conscious choice to commit to one another and to share of themselves; trust is not something that we dish out lightly to one another.

Privacy

There is a very fine balance between privacy and openness within a partnership. How much privacy are we entitled to? Why would you consider excluding the person with whom you have chosen to share your life from an important aspect of your life? You should be able to trust each other enough to feel that you need not hide things from one another. Forming a healthy relationship with oneself and the other should take priority over one's selfish personal needs. Whatever we aspire to in our relationships will all fall into place when we are giving and receiving love and support to ourselves and the other.

Suspicion

When you first become aware of a possible betrayal, it is important to take a step back and consider whether your initial premise was sound. Did it really happen, or did your suspicious mind create the betrayal? Maybe you are over-reacting because you are feeling insecure or tired. Maybe you're adding other abuses to this situation.

Although the feeling of being lied to evokes a knee-jerk emotional response in anyone, it is vital to stay rational. You need to focus on the facts and avoid the fiction. Try as much as possible *not* to become disempowered by the situation, and make a conscious effort *not* to participate in the other person's bad behaviour. Essentially, their lie is not your problem. They created it and they have to live with it. Take their negative emotion, peel it off of yourself, and release it back to them.

It often helps to verbalise while doing this, "I recognise that I have this feeling, I will look at it, remove it from myself, and send it back to where it came from." Send it back with love and not with anger. You do not need to share the load created by someone else's fear. The more of their stuff you take on, the less opportunity you give them to deal with their baggage.

There are at least two people involved in any betrayal. Firstly, you betray yourself – and secondly, you betray another. Most people say that it was not the act behind the lie that left them feeling gutted; it was the fact that their partner did not respect them enough to be honest.

Deception can't be measured in degrees on a scale from one to ten. If your partner says, "I have a late meeting again tonight," and you discover that these meetings are, in fact, sneak trips to a strip club, it will not pacify you to have a friend say, "That's nothing. Mine's much worse. At least yours isn't having an affair." Deception is deception and comparing different forms of it doesn't make you feel any better. You were kept in the dark, and in the dark it all feels the same. Whether your partner was lying about their habitual casino visits, meeting a lover, or indulging in a drug fix – you were deliberately excluded from an integral part of their life. Trust and respect are essential in any relationship, and betrayal breaks them both. The question you need to ask yourself is: is it possible to trust this person again? Unfortunately, their behaviour can become habitual and it will probably happen again.

When betrayal happens more than once, it always comes as a shock – even if you were warned that the chances are high that it would. Especially if you sat down with your partner and discussed the situation – if you both agreed to work on the relationship and to be open with one another – and then discover that the deception hasn't stopped. Unfortunately, their need to be somewhere else, doing something else (without you) is more important than being with you. If they are addicts, their primary relationship will be with gambling, sex, substances and so on. You will always come second until they decide to seriously commit to making a lifestyle change. Those individuals who don't have the courage to leave a redundant relationship – or who can't face the idea of a failed relationship – will resort to home or partner avoidance. In doing this, they deny telling themselves the truth and therefore can't be honest with others either.

Sixth sense

Usually, one has a sixth sense about deception. This is especially true when people share space. We learn to read certain behaviour changes and other unconscious cues such as intangible shifts in intimacy in our partner. When the truth eventually emerges, and it will, the relationship can never be the same again because there will be no clear boundary between truth and lies. The relationship essentially loses its innocence. If someone intentionally and successfully managed to betray your trust in the past, what would stop them from doing so again? It is their habit because they are unable to live with the consequences of speaking their truth. Sometimes people say, "I couldn't tell you because I didn't want to hurt you." The truth may cause acute pain for a while, but lying is worse since it always results in chronic mistrust and long-term pain.

And then the questions start. "Where did they meet?" "Do they know each other?" "What happened in the past; what is happening now?"

"What is wrong with me?" "Why did she hide her addiction problems from me; or was I just too blind to see?" We start to question everything and all the time spent together begins to feel meaningless and false. All those occasions that you suspected something was amiss will resurface to haunt you now – times when you suspected something but cancelled out your feelings of uneasiness. The relationship will look very different now, and so will your partner. Do you really know who this person is? Did you ever really know them? Do you want to waste so much of your valuable energy and time trying to work out the answers to your questions, or worrying about the next possible betrayal?

Cheating

Another type of betrayal is cheating. Cheating happens in many types of relationships – business relationships, personal relationship, and friendships. We all know of someone who is having an affair while in a committed relationship; or someone who is talking behind a friend's back; or someone planning a shady business deal. Interestingly, if one randomly interviewed people about the concept of cheating, they would say that cheating is unacceptable. Why? Because most of us desire respect within our relationships. We all want to be in the picture. We do not want to be the one who is being taken for a ride.

What constitutes cheating or betrayal? When you form a relationship contract, it is a good idea to outline what you would define as cheating. Obviously having an affair is the most commonly cited behaviour. But would you say your wife or girlfriend was cheating on you if she kissed another woman? Is your male partner cheating on you if he is paying to have anonymous sex with a prostitute once a month? If someone is secretly going online and masturbating over some website, would that be as unappealing to you as finding out that they had been intimate with someone at the office for the past year?

Blaming inner urges is no excuse for cheating in any type of relationship. Everyone has urges, and everyone also has a choice to refrain from acting on those urges. If you are being unfaithful because you have commitment issues or an inferiority complex, rather stay single until you feel ready and worthy to commit to a relationship.

Sometimes we are attracted to how someone is when they are in a relationship with someone else. They look and sound good to us; they seem to have it all. However, once that person is removed from that particular relationship and is inserted into your life, they start to look different because we all bring out different qualities in different people. We encourage them to express different aspects of themselves (both positive and negative) by being who we are. We need to be realistic about what is happening 'out there' and start to value what we have 'in here.'

If you know that your partner is having an affair, the primary question still remains: Is this affair maintaining your committed relationship or your marriage? You know that your partner is cheating on you, but you have decided that the other perks associated with your relationship are too good to lose. Do you find it useful to meet with your friends who are in the same boat and spend time plotting how to fleece your partners financially? Or would you rather engage in similar behaviour, because you *think* that this will make the other feel the same sense of betrayal you are feeling?

Or, you may also start doing things behind your partner's back to gain some sort of secret advantage, so that when they do something that hurts you, you have this stash of ammunition. Actually, this won't shoot them down; it merely pacifies your insecurities. This covert behaviour indicates that you are also not totally committed to sharing in the relationship – and this exacerbates a non-committal response in your partner. Your behaviour is being reflected back to you and theirs to them. No behaviour happens in isolation. This cold war circumstance causes illness, unhappiness and stress, for both of you. It reflects your relationship with yourself. How do you betray yourself by letting yourself down? If you lie to yourself, others will lie to you. What you do to another, you do to yourself. And how you treat yourself is how others will treat you.

Secrecy usually causes a lot of stress for the person engaging in it because at some stage the affair may start to threaten their committed relationship. Your partner may become suspicious, or the affair partner will want more. If you are cheating on someone, can you maintain your self-respect and your integrity? Do you really think that others will not look at you and think, "If he can do this to her, can I trust him in a business deal?" Or, "If she is deceiving her partner, can she be trusted in her position at work or as a friend?" The cheating lifestyle that you create turns into a reward, guilt and blame game – and it ends up defining who you are.

Anyone can cheat – it is easy and there are plenty of opportunities. However, there is no such thing as having one's proverbial bread buttered on both sides in the long term. Ironically, you not only lose your partner in the process, you lose yourself as well. So, be truthful with yourself and others. Have the courage to break away from an unsatisfactory relationship and commit to forming a decent one with yourself instead. This applies both to the betrayer and the betrayed.

Sharing resources

What are your issues relating to sharing? How were you taught to understand money as a child? Did it symbolise freedom for you? How often did your thoughts turn to, "When I leave home I will earn my own money and be free?" Did you constantly hear, "If only we had money this could happen or that could be done?" Were you trained to believe that money solved problems?

Did your caregivers use money and material things as pacifiers because they did not make the time to nurture you emotionally? Were you given material things as a demonstration of love?

Freedom and money can become linked through our early learning experiences, and lack of money will therefore be viewed as a trap. We can also learn that love equals money, "I know he loves me because he bought me this." However, it is just paper – like the leaves falling from a tree to fertilize the ground to feed the new growth in spring. It is a cycle; do not interfere or become fearful of this flow. Money is a form of energy and it is infinite when we do not fixate on it. The *love* of money really is the root of all evil, not the money itself.

Having money can enhance your happiness *only* if you already know what happiness looks and feels like. When love goes out of a relationship, money becomes a problem. Money becomes the focus.

"He does not love me enough or give me the attention I want, so I will take his credit card and go shopping. I have to get something out of this relationship."

It is *not* true that when money goes out the back door, love will automatically diminish. Love that is based on something real can withstand a change in material fortune and may even deepen as a result of having to pull together to get through the difficulty. However, if love is based on something false, such as money or the lifestyle that money can buy, it stands to reason that love will survive for only as long as the money does; the money is keeping the love alive.

When love, sharing, and commitment are present within a relationship, the possibilities are endless. It is an old cliché, but money cannot buy you love. Money can pacify emptiness. It could become your primary relationship – a substitute for what you do not have – and it can eventually become an extension of your identity. People will like you for your money because that is who you are.

Poverty consciousness

Why have we learned to associate wealth with money? Is someone with a strong structure of community support less wealthy than someone with pseudo-friends who only keep company with them because they have money? People often feel deprived in environments in which there are different levels of having and not-having. They live their lives by comparison. They want to have all the nice things that they *think* the rich person up on the hill has. They want to *be* that person. What they do not consider are all the problems that person has; and they forget what they already have. Nothing material will ever make you someone you are not. And, no-one actually has anything – we are all just renting while we are here on earth.

What is important is what you carry within you to the life hereafter; and the contributions that you make by being who you are while you are here. When you are ill and bedridden, what would you choose?
A. People pushing money under your bedroom door
B. Many friends bringing you soup and companionship

What is poverty alleviation?

People can be raised out of poverty only if they choose to change their paradigm and start empowering themselves. Governments throw money at poverty because they want the problem to go away. They do not care about the people, they only want their votes. But money cannot change a mindset. It just creates more disempowerment because those people who are given hand-outs become more dependent on being rescued, and more accustomed to being labelled and identified as being poor – and so the cycle perpetuates.

Never wait for someone to give you back your dignity – they do not even know they have it. It is your responsibility to find your dignity, reclaim it, and own it.

In some instances, people are ostracised because they try to uplift themselves. Their own friends will make attempts to bring them down and criticise them for being ambitious and for wanting a change. Society prefers predictable sheep rather than encouraging freedom from the herd. People are much easier to control if they conform to a common reality – a consensus reality. As soon as we start questioning what we are taught to believe, we are labeled rebellious or on the fringe because we choose not to conform to the norm. When someone questions the common reality, others may feel insecure. We find safety in doing what has always been done. We also tend to support one another's failures because it's what we're all used to. Sometimes jealousy of someone's success can be so intense that it leads to physical harm being done to the person. If you are in a situation like this, make new friends. The friendships that you have are most likely conditional and damaging. And conditional friendship is not friendship at all.

What do you choose? Do you want the support of a community? Or do you prefer to isolate yourself and have more material wealth? Does having many true friends make you wealthier than someone with loads of money who is lonely and unloved? The more you share, the more you will have; what you sow, you will reap.

What is your relationship with money? Do you fear it? Are you greedy for it; and do you hoard it? Do you lose sleep over it? It's just paper with numbers on … tree … leaves … compost … leaves. You will always have enough, but maybe you don't know what enough is. Learn to want what you have rather than have what you want.

WHEN RELATIONSHIPS END

ക്കരു

I bring to you the message of letting go ... of graciously accepting the message and allowing the process to flow.

ക്കരു

We all have different responses to the end of a relationship. And our response depends very much on how the relationship ended, who initiated the end and – if it wasn't us – whether we agreed to end the relationship or not. Sometimes we know early on that a relationship won't last, but we persevere in the hope that he or she will become what we envision them to be. We overlook the signs and think, "They will change. This is not who they really are." We stay in a relationship in the hope that it will become what we want it to be; because we reflect on the feelings that we had when we met – and we wait for that initial euphoria to return.

But many relationships do end. They reach a point where they no longer serve either partner. They become tired and need to be put to rest and, ideally, we should let go and allow this to happen. But, how many of us do? How comfortable do you feel releasing something in which you invested much of yourself, your time, your hopes and your emotions? Because of this, even when you know your relationships is dead, you hang on in denial and complain about your partner. And if they pick up the signs and choose to leave, you are upset and you want to punish them for deserting you.

Realistically, it is futile to pursue a relationship with someone once they have decided that it is over. They have moved on and we have no right to hold them back. If a relationship is to be salvaged, it requires a firm commitment from both parties to do so. Each person must desire the relationship for the relationship's sake, not for the children, or property, or convenience.

Relationships do not end only when you are no longer seen as a couple (or in case of a friendship, when you are no longer perceived as friends). Relationships can be over when you are still together. And when the end is in sight, it becomes your choice to stay or to move on. Most of us don't like goodbyes and we resist the change because it feels uncomfortable and unfamiliar. We think we might be making a mistake by leaving, even though our emotional needs are not being met. We make an effort to avoid the other by spending more time away from them.

What happened to us?

An ending doesn't mean that there is something wrong with you or with your partner. You are simply not compatible anymore; you've stopped bringing out the best in each other. You have moved in different directions, and the reason you got together in the first place is no longer valid. Staying together therefore no longer serves a purpose. Interestingly, there are both good and bad reasons for ending a relationship.

Good reasons would be:
- You are involved with someone who is too controlling and you feel as if you need to compromise your values and belief systems to be accepted by them. You have lost too much of your identity to remain in the relationship.
- Your partner is unreasonably jealous.
- Abuse in any form.
- You argue most of the time.
- There is no intimacy or affection. You are not there for each other.
- You are being cheated on or betrayed or you are doing the cheating.
- You are trying to resuscitate a dead relationship.

Bad reasons would be:

- An unwillingness to address the real reasons behind the problems that are highlighted when you are in a relationship with anyone.
- Not accepting the message or learning the lessons the relationship brought you by choosing to play the victim and blaming and shaming the other. Your unresolved issues will be repeated in your next relationship.
- Angry manipulative threats of "It's over," and then staying away for a week or two only to return. This ends up becoming a hire-and-fire relationship; a game. Be sure that you want it to end and stand by your decision.
- Someone else is telling you to leave and you're doing it to please them.

What now?

When the end of a relationship arrives, we may be totally unable to see the possibility of life without this person – or the possibility of other relationships – because our entire focus is still stuck in the past. We are still glued to the lost relationship and suddenly all we can see are the perfect parts. We are really good at remembering the positives when we are faced with a loss, but while we are in the relationship all we do is review the negatives.

Often much of our self-worth is invested in gaining a certain response and receiving acknowledgement from our relationship partner. We may also need to be in a relationship to feel secure and acceptable, to feel as if we belong somewhere, because we are satisfying a social expectation. When a relationship ends, our worthiness and our role die with it and we have to start rebuilding our self identity after the breakup.

We affect one another

It is worthwhile noting that the end of a relationship affects both partners because both have to deal with change. The degree to which you are negatively affected will depend on how much of your identity you retained within the shared environment. If your definition of self was derived from your partnership, you will experience greater difficulty establishing yourself as a singleton. If you were very dependent on your partner, you possibly have co-dependency issues that will exacerbate your loss once the relationship disintegrates. Were you defined by your partner or your relationship? And now that it is over, who are you?

As with any loss, you should allow yourself a grieving period to get over the shock and the trauma. You are no longer in a partnership, you possibly lost your role identity (and maybe a home, children, mutual friends and family). Your way of life is different now, and your comfort zone (however uncomfortable it might have become) is gone. This leaves a void in your life – a gap that could be filled with self-doubt, disappointment, anger, and possibly depression.

There are no rules for how long it takes to get over a relationship, so give yourself the time you need without slipping into self-pity or vengefulness. Consider what you learned through being part of the relationship. Remember to honour the messenger who came into your life to teach you about yourself.

Reviewing history

If you are struggling to come to terms with the loss and are giving too much attention to the fear that you may never find another partner, it may be useful to write down your relationship history (in detail) to remind yourself that there were past relationships and that there will be others in the future. Every time a relationship ended and you felt devastated, someone new did appear in time. When your eyes are no longer clouded over with visions of your ex, you will see new opportunities. Do you own your life or was he or she your *life's work*? Are you at a loss because you were an extension of someone else's experience?

When you review your relationship history, do you find common factors in the way each relationship ended?

- Why did the relationships end? What has been the primary cause?
- What were the signs leading up to each break-up?
- What was the trigger, the last straw? Has this happened before?

145

- Do you find yourself arguing about the same things in all your relationships?
- Who ended it and are the reasons similar to the last time?

Making space for better things

If you end a relationship for the right reasons, you will be rewarded. You will have the time and space to nurture your self-worth and to start enjoying your own company. The longer you keep someone in your space for the wrong reasons, the less likely you are to grow and know what type of person and relationship is good for you.

There are common universal principles found in all good relationships, whether the relationship is romantic, professional, or platonic. A very important aspect is a willingness to give. If someone is more focused on getting than giving, they are selfish and this creates resentment in the other. A good relationship also gives us a safe environment in which to grow as a person; it challenges our stuckness. If we learn to listen to each other with understanding, practice open communication, and let go of our need to be right, we can contribute tremendously in creating a relationship that benefits both partners.

However, if you remain surrounded by people whom you've outgrown, or who do not relate to who you are, nothing will change for you until you decide to move on. By remaining where you are, you are ensuring that you only attract more of the same. No-one new and different can get in as they feel that they do not 'fit in' with your circumstances as they stand. Your space is cluttered with people you have possibly outgrown but *think* you still need. If you are staying in a relationship because it is *better than nothing* you are damaging yourself. Your security blanket will likely end up suffocating you.

Every time you let go of a circumstance that does not support your highest good, you will make space for new and inspirational experiences. Before moving on, review your history and your relationship behaviour. If you are still sending out the same message, you will still attract the same type of person. What do you really want? Is the message you send out congruent with who you are or do you send mixed messages? It is very important that your thoughts and your actions are aligned. If your actions say that you are free and easy and independent and love to have a good time, but your thoughts are wishing for a stable, committed relationship, you will draw what you present to the outside world. Your message will be, "I'm available and don't like to be stuck with one person. I like to socialise with many others." And the person you attract will be what you asked for.

Many hundreds of years ago Aristotle was quoted as saying that "nature abhors a vacuum." Matter fills up the natural world and when one thing is removed, it is soon replaced by another. Human nature appears to be the same. We don't enjoy having a vacuum in our lives and as soon as a significant other leaves, we set about trying to fill the space left by them with another person, sometimes *any* person. However, if we choose to fill the space with ourselves instead, we would give ourselves a wonderful opportunity to review, understand and evolve our relationship with ourselves to the next level. If we do not give ourselves the space to get to know ourselves again, we will fill the gap with exactly the same type of person we had before. They may have a different face and wear different clothes, but their message will essentially be the same.

Therefore, do not make irrational choices based on fear. Accept that you will never be alone; that there will always be others who would like to move into your vacuum. Rather than simply filling the void, use this opportunity to form new friendships and enjoy exploring your potential as an individual. Let go of the idea that only one person is good for you and start forming good platonic relationships.

We are complex beings and we need more than just one person to be our mirror. It is unfair of us to burden one person with all of our expectations and our experiments at growth. If we do it with fairness, we can strive to have deep friendships and a central relationship all at the same time. We can have *both-and* instead of *either-or* but to do so we need firm boundaries in place. Our relationship with ourselves must be intact. Go out and find others who can show you different sides of yourself, and for whom you can do the same. Find people you can talk and laugh with; people who uncover your joy. Magical encounters can happen in a fleeting moment. You don't have to take anyone and everyone home with you.

Reviewing themes and patterns

You will be attracted to the same type of relationship until your particular lesson is learned. Mostly, we need to learn to love and respect ourselves – to see ourselves as worthy of being loved. Sometimes we need to be shown how to live our lives without feeling guilty and overly responsible for others. You might find it useful to make a note of all your past relationships – whatever level they were on – and spot the common denominator.

The non-committal type

Did you attract the non-committal type? If so, you should investigate your own ability to commit. Do not blame others before considering what attracted you to their behaviour in the first place. Consider that you may not trust the concept of commitment yourself; you may feel safer knowing that you cannot lose what you never had. So you choose commitment-phobic relationships to feel safe. If someone made a commitment to you, would you possibly leave them?

The messenger is saying, *"Look at your issues regarding commitment. Can you commit?"*

The narcissist

Narcissists teach us that we too have rights. They specialise in themselves. The narcissist has an unhealthy ego manifestation, but you are drawn to their arrogance because you do not know what you want or who you are. They will tell you. When this ego-person shines their light on you, you feel alive, and when they ignore you, you die. What you need to learn is that you have a right to your own needs and to your own choices. Do not martyr yourself for someone else's cause. It is not selfish to know what you want, it is the intent with which you carry out your actions that is important. There is a huge difference between fulfilling your needs in a loving, respectful manner and doing this out of greed or need with no awareness of others. You do not need to be the little dog sitting under the dinner table waiting for scraps; being only occasionally allowed to sit at the table. Stop working so hard at being 'good enough' to get that little bit of attention from another, and start to give yourself the attention you deserve.

The messenger is saying, *"Find your worthiness. Who are you?"*

The needy

Do people often say, "Why do you always end up with people who are not good enough for you?" Often these are the needy, spongy types you've ended up with. They expect you to do everything for them. You may have to support them financially (even pay their debts), or provide accommodation, or manage their lives because they are addicts. This is like adopting a child. Why would you do this? Relationships are meant to be about mutual sharing between adults, not raising an adolescent. Review your own need issues – is it important that someone needs you so that they will never leave you? This is not a good enough reason to be in a relationship. And they are likely to leave you if they find a better sponsor anyway.

The messenger is saying, *"Take care of yourself first. Only then are you able to take care of another."*

The abuser

Not all abusers resort to physical means to gain control over their partners. They can also use emotional and economic means. Abuse can happen in heterosexual and same-sex relationships and the aim is to gain power over the other. They want to be your boss. Whatever form the abuse takes, the outcome is the same – you are left feeling worthless and undervalued. You feel as if you are to blame for the relationship breakdown, and you will probably think that you can fix it. You can't. If you are being manipulated financially, or bruised physically, or humiliated and intimidated emotionally, you need to ask yourself why you feel that you deserve this form of attention – and why you allow it to continue. What is the benefit in it for you?

The messenger is saying, *"Love is not pain and pain is not love."*

Too independent

Do you choose to become involved with people who are too independent and self-sufficient? Some people fear entering a relationship because they think they will lose themselves and their identity. Their need to maintain their individuality is so strong that it becomes very difficult to build a relationship and a life with them. Where do you fit in with someone like this? Can you share your space, your feelings, and your wishes with someone who always wants to do everything for themselves and dislikes asking for your help?

The messenger is saying, *"Look at your boundaries and your ability to say 'no' when others need you."*

Picky and critical

Picky people often criticise themselves as much as they criticise others. They demand a lot from everything but tend to focus on the negatives – to see what's wrong and bad in every situation. If you keep choosing this type of partner, how many joyful experiences do you have with them?

The messenger is saying, *"Stop trying to be perfect for someone else."*

But what if it's you?

But what if *you* are the narcissist? Have you ever considered how un-attractive your selfish behaviour is? Or if you are the abuser; are you aware of how blatant your fear is to others? Would you stay with someone if they treated you like this? Have your relationships ended because you are too independent; or are you too needy? What are you reflecting in your partner and vice versa; and are you willing to get the message and learn the lesson?

People on the outside often have a much clearer picture of us and our relationship choices than we do, so it is worthwhile listening to their opinions. If you are choosing undeserving partners, it means that you feel you do not deserve to be loved and respected. You feel that they deserve your love and attention more than you do, and so you end up neglecting yourself.

What type of relationship is comfortable for you, and what is your zone of familiarity? How would you define your relationships – as healthy or unhealthy? Can you say that your relationship brings you joy and supports your self-worth? If not, it is time to make some big changes!

Singleness

It is very important to spend a certain percentage of your life as a single, uncommitted person. This special time gives you the opportunity to learn to enjoy your own company, and to become resourceful at finding those things that inspire you.

If you are single, make the effort to take yourself out. Do not stay in the same environment every day and every weekend. Your thoughts will go round and around and end up nowhere. Join interest groups or clubs that are productive and that have a positive impact on you.

You need to come to know that you are okay doing things for yourself and by yourself. Find out who your friends are; and form good, solid and supportive relationships with them. Choose the right people and give and receive mutually to one another. You do not need to be surrounded by many others. A few true friends are worth more than you will ever imagine, so invest in them. Singleness is a great time to practice the basics of all relationships – without the sex.

Me-time

Single time is your opportunity to do everything that you have ever wanted to do. You can travel, study, go out with many different people and not be accountable (within reason) to anyone except yourself. You can explore your creativity and create a sacred space for yourself. This is a time to fully experience how to be in a relationship with yourself so that you really know who you are and what it is that keeps your heart open.

The risk of singleness is that we can start becoming selfish about 'me-stuff' and rigid protective boundaries can emerge. Or we may become like a hermit, never going out and living vicariously through books and DVDs. This is not healthy in the long term as it can lead to isolation and depression. Humans are tribal, sociable beings and having social interactions and experiencing a sense of belonging are very important to our wellbeing.

However, some people do function better single than they do paired up, and that is fine. We all need to decide what works best for us and how we achieve our peace and our inspiration. If we do choose to be in a relationship, it should be because we have a desire to share and to love and be loved, not because we are scared of being alone. Learn, also, to get the same feeling from sharing time with friends as you do when you are with your relationship partner. If you enjoy being single, stay that way. There are no rules on how we need to be, so long as we are in harmony with ourselves.

Relationship with your past

Ideally we should honour the interconnectedness of all our relationships. Make friends with your past experiences and retain the good from each one. Every incident and interaction has contributed to who you are now and how you respond and behave in each new relationship.

Are you stuck in a present circumstance that is disturbing a past sore point? Are you constantly being reminded of your past? Remember that a wound cannot heal if you keep picking at the scabs.

If you did things that make you feel uncomfortable or guilty, make a conscious decision to forgive yourself. Also, forgive yourself for not treating yourself with kindness. We all need to learn; but we do not need to make the same mistakes repeatedly. If it feels less stimulating trying to get the same feeling out of doing something, you have outgrown it – so move on. Stop doing things that worked in the past that are clearly not working now. We need to move forward and create new experiences instead of designing a copy-and-paste life.

If you keep trying to re-create the past, ask yourself, "*What is wrong with the present?*" Why do you find it safer to live in the past, as you were then, than living in the present? Maybe you feel that you have lost the attention and affirmation that you had then, and you need to get that feeling back again. In the past, did you rely on your physical attractiveness, being the drunk-party-animal with wild stories, or being the one who always told the jokes? Sadly, we do seem to regress to perceived happy times when we are feeling insecure. If you are missing the past, consider what it is about this past of yours that you really want to return to.

Objectively review how your behaviour impacts on your current environment. What are the consequences? Are you happy with having the same image you had as a teenager? We need to remember that trying to please others and looking for external validation can become embarrassing as we age. Authenticity should be prioritised, and you should be forming a fair idea of who you are now. People move on and there will always be younger and better-looking heroes and heroines filling the social environment – so do not try to act 'out there' anymore. You will not feel fulfilled.

Redefine your relationship with yourself. What is important to you now? There is no point in being able to relate only to who you were then, or who you will be one day. The now, which is the most important building block for tomorrow, should be where you place your attention. What type of foundations are you really laying? What and who you were then is over and it belongs in the past. Things change all the time. Life is a living being that we continuously recreate and co-create. Find your true flow and go with it.

Relationship with your ex

Does your ex still push your buttons? Does he or she still create some sort of uncomfortable response within you when you see them or hear what they have been up to? Who do you become when you are confronted by an ex? And is there possibly unfinished business in that relationship?

Very often much of what we feel is determined by who ended the relationship, as well as the reason it dissolved. We are also affected by the amount of self-worth that we invested in being with that person. We may feel some regret, especially if we perceive them to be smarter and better and more successful than we remember them; and now we feel we have lost the opportunity to be with someone like that. However, we are not necessarily missing *that* particular person, but rather what they represent. The reality is that they have moved on. They are as they are now because they are no longer in a relationship with you. If you had to get back with him or her, you would find that nothing between the two of you will be the same because of the change and growth that happened after the separation. It's not possible to have the same relationship with them ever again.

In some relationships, we are 'trained' to be on edge. Our partner may make us feel unworthy or insecure, or they may have awakened a fear within us about something. They could provoke childhood issues, or press our buttons of rejection and loss. When we see them, we feel disempowered because we – for whatever reason – chose to surrender our feeling of wholeness to them. We gave them control. After the relationship ends and you bump into them, your memory will say, "What have I done wrong; what is wrong with me?" because you have stored their face with that feeling. That is part of your unfinished business – to reclaim the parts of yourself that you gave to your ex, and to reassemble yourself to feel whole again despite that.

You may also notice that after a break-up, he again became the person with whom you fell in love when you first met. But why did he change into something different when he was in a relationship with you? Did he perhaps feel too inhibited to express himself with you in the relationship? Or, is he simply very good at marketing himself initially and then he turns into someone different later? If that is so, you fell in love with an illusion; something that you *wanted* to believe in.

Do you find yourself saying, "How can his life just carry on now that he's devastated mine?" Why did you let him own your life? Were you something because of him? Did he make you feel alive? Remember to say to yourself, "I am someone who is worthy in spite of him," and let go of past relationships – because that is where they belong; in the past. You do not have to plug yourself into another person in order to access joyfulness. It is freely available to everyone. Release those past people with love, because their time in your life has clearly run its course and it is time to rediscover fresh and different aspects of yourself and of your life.

Relationship with self

How often have you considered having a relationship with yourself? Usually when we think of relationships, we visualise a partner, an external person. But what of the internal person – you?

It has often been said that you cannot love another until you love yourself. Do you? Mostly, we neglect giving to ourselves because we think that if we give to others first, we will find what we are looking for in that other. This leaves us feeling empty. We have nothing to offer another because loving ourselves is the gift that we have to give the world. If we don't love ourselves, we can't expect anyone else to love us either. If you find yourself falling in and out of love trying to fill a gap, consider filling that space with you. Once you do discover a way of relating to yourself, giving becomes a conscious experience and not a knee-jerk response to some unknown stimulus.

Who are you? Who you *want* to be or who you *think* you are do not necessarily correlate with who you *actually* are. How would you define yourself on your own without any social constructs, associations, or titles to support your definition? If you were stranded somewhere in isolation, away from societal organograms, and a voice from the ethers asked you, *"Can you describe what your soul looks like? What is your essence? How do you hold that which sits deep within your heart like a soft pearl waiting to be nurtured?"* What would you say?

Do you treat yourself with kindness, or are you self-punitive? How much guilt do you carry? Is it guilt over past wrongs you have done to others, or is it a sense of misplaced guilt that you feel when you do things *just for me* because you believe that you do not deserve good things, that you only have a right to something if everyone else is OK? Why is this so? Do you want to jump into the bottomless pit with your partner? Will this solve anything? How can you help them if you are stuck down there in the mud with them?

If you are drawn to chaos, check your internal levels of anarchy, your emotional status. If you are out of touch with yourself, you will be attracted to an intense external environment, such as addictions to sex, drugs, gambling, and volatile relationships. And if you are addicted, ask yourself whether you are you trying to control the external environment to feel more fixed internally?

The fuzzy zone

If you were raised in a household where you were not encouraged to have your own sense of identity or to develop your own personality, you will experience serious difficulty knowing who you are. This will become especially apparent in relationships where you share space. You may find yourself saying, "I lose myself in relationships; when I'm single I'm a different person. When this relationship ends I'll be able to get back to doing the things I want to do."

This happens especially if you choose a relationship that mimics your early childhood home. Unconsciously, you will feel as if you are under someone else's roof again, and you will remember how you were not allowed to live out your life for fear of being punished. Your adult home situation turns you into a child again and you become re-anaesthetised to your right to live your life *now*. You will end up trying to do everything perfectly for the other, and living your life for them. And you might even follow their instructions because that is how you were accepted as a child. You will do anything to avoid rejection, even if it means sabotaging yourself.

Comparison

Some people like to define themselves through comparison with others. They need the external environment to give them clues about who they are; and their centre of measurement is dependent on validation from this environment. They may make statements like, "At least I've got a job. There are others with nothing." The measurement of what you perceive as success will be by comparison. "Compared with John, I'm quite lucky; he might have a nice house, but he hates his job."

Show me my ID

Interestingly, you can never *be* the other person who you appoint as the gold-standard measurement for your life. Also, you will never really know what goes on in every aspect of their life and you will see only what you want to see; that which suits you. You will choose the aspects of a person that you see as desirable, and then try to align yourself with those traits because you believe others will then see you in that light too.

But basing your self-acceptance on the degree of acknowledgement you receive from others is futile and irrelevant. Your self-identity will never be stable, as you have delegated it to outsiders who do not necessarily realise they have this responsibility. The end result is usually a fragmented personality. You may even find that you end up acting different roles with different people on different occasions.

If you find yourself trying to insert yourself into a community or group with a strong sense of identity to gain appreciation and acceptance, it is possible that you need outside influences to define you. When you travel to a foreign country, do you immediately start conforming to their cultural dress and traditions, at the expense of your own, just to feel that you belong? Are you someone who needs a community or peer group outside the one you were born into to define you? It may be that you have chosen a way that you admire and you want to become like them in order to find your personal definition of self. "Look at me. I'm just like you, can't you see?" But they cannot give you the validation you need on your behalf, and neither can anyone else.

If you need the outside world to define you, it is possible that somewhere during your formative years you never developed a structured internal idea of who you are. And now in your adult years, you need to look outside for pointers – some indication of where you could belong and how to *be*. Your basic need is to conform to something so that you can belong somewhere. Because you do not know who you inherently are, you therefore choose to take your identity from a herd that you admire.

How do you define yourself? Is this who you really are, or this who you would like to be?

- Which group do you align with? Is it the group in which you were raised? If not, why are you rejecting your roots?
- Do you try to be like someone else? Who is this person – and why would you want to be a copy of someone else's image?

- Do you extrapolate your identity from another culture – one other than your birthright? What is it about your birth identity that you reject?
- Where are your roots? Can you comfortably stand your ground?

Dig up your roots

Explore your family tree to know and understand your roots. Find out how your ancestors behaved, and what they did. Where did they live, and what were their relationship choices? You have fragments of their genes inside of you at the most basic level of your existence.

- Do you experience déjà vu in certain cities or in some situations?
- Were these perhaps places where your ancestors lived or visited once upon a time?
- Are you making similar decisions and acting out similar behaviours to your forefathers?

The one aspect we cannot escape is that we inherit the genes of our forefathers. The blessing is that we have free will and can choose whether we want to become like them or not. We can accept or reject our inheritance. We can choose to get cancer because everyone else in the family line developed this condition, or we can behave differently. We can break the multi-generational cycle on all levels – body, mind and spirit. You can make a conscious decision not to think and live in ways that you know are negative and hopeless. We do not need to unconsciously perpetuate the sins of our forefathers. It is vital to break out of bad training and programming or anything else that leaves you feeling like a victim. Reclaim your personal power, it is your birthright.

Authenticity

How authentic are you? Do you speak your truth and fulfill your ideals? Do those around you know you as you know yourself, or do you hide things from others for fear of rejection? If you are not comfortable expressing who you truly are, this means that you are self-rejecting – a chronic form of self-sabotage. It is slow suicide. You will never be truly peaceful if you live in denial of yourself by living beside yourself.

When you have an internal centre of control, you are able to feel comfortable defining yourself without the need for direction from others. You will not need to draw attention to yourself or make silly jokes to feel useful. Your *right to be* will not be determined by the acceptance of others, and therefore you will not feel unworthy just by *being*. You are your own gold standard and you compete against yourself. You are not better or worse off than someone else – you are just who you are, how you are, where you are; and that is where you belong.

Being comfortable in your own skin

How do you treat your body? Do you nurture yourself or harm yourself? Were you trained to gain acceptance through your appearance? How much of your self-worth is invested in your looks? You will know you are over-invested in your physical appearance if you spend too much time focusing on preening, grooming, and toning. If you feel that you look unattractive, how does this affect your mood and your behaviour? Do you get into a bad mood if your hair is on strike, or if your jeans feel too tight? When all these uncomfortable feelings arise, what do you wear and what do you do? Do you choose an item of clothing to draw attention to other parts of your body that you think might *work* for you? Why is being *you* not enough? How do you cope with the fact that you are ageing?

And what about being in the body that you are. If a boy is raised by a single mother who is often involved in unhappy relationships, he will learn that men are bad because they cause his mother pain. He will start aligning himself with women and reject himself as a man, as he does not want to be associated with the group that is causing his mother to suffer. This can result in self-sabotaging behaviour later on in life – not overt – often a work addiction, where he works himself to death to prove his worthiness, to re-establish his right to be who he is.

Women can also reject their femininity if they were raised in an environment in which women were referred to as dumb and men as clever. This message can create a double-bind situation for a young girl who is intelligent, but is programmed to believe that in order to be acceptable she has to be sexy and helpless. This means that no matter what she does, she loses. She is as intelligent as a man, but she is stuck in a woman's body – should she risk expressing her intelligence and face rejection because of it?

Thoughts

Are your mind and body in harmony? Do you like to think and create? Maybe the internal dialogue of your thoughts keeps you awake at night. And if it does, what do you do with your thoughts in those dark hours to still the chatter? If you spend a lot of time expecting the worst and creating scenarios of fear and impossibility, that is how your life will be – fearful and impossible. You are more likely to develop high blood pressure, bad moods and insomnia. Remember, an obstacle does not always have to be overcome – maybe you should try looking to the left or right of it for the answers and the opportunities. Do not take everything so personally – it is usually not about you. Often we need to step back when we are insulted and criticized to see what's really happening; that the verbal attack aimed at us is actually a reflection of what's happening inside the other.

Do you enjoy the versatility of your mind, or do you use it only to escape into studying when emotions are too overwhelming? Do you find that being in the mental plane is safer than being in touch with your emotions? Are you one of those people who choose information as your primary relationship to stay cerebral? Do you find yourself looking for a fresh course or a new study distraction when your relationship becomes too overbearing? Or, have you perhaps based your self-worth on your achievements because you fail at achieving good relationship results? "I am worthy because I scored 80% in my exam."

Everything is good for you so long as what you think and what you feel translate into a healthy expression of yourself. Your body can send messages back to your mind to say that you feel okay, and your mind can remind your body to hold the stillness. It is the intent with which we carry out our actions that gives us the clues about our relationship with ourselves. It is *how* we do what we do that is important. As long as you feel that what you are thinking is pure, and that you are centred and peaceful with your world, all is well and you are on track.

It is a basic Universal Law that what you give will be returned to you – and you will attract more of the same. To what do you give all your energy? Whatever that is, you will become it; you give life to whatever you choose to give your attention to. So become more of what you want to receive and achieve in the world.

Pain points

When we start out in this life, we are connected to spirit and are dependent on our environment for nurturing and safety. As we grow, we become aware of ourselves as separate physical individuals through emotional pain and feelings. We also have interactive experiences with our environment – we learn cognitively and become conditioned to what we need to do to give us the greatest feelings of security. We do not always have to learn through pain, but it is those uncomfortable feelings that draw our attention to issues that we should be dealing with. Pain points us to the issues that need our attention.

Look to your history of disease and notice the patterns throughout your life. If you had certain ailments (for example asthma or other respiratory conditions) in childhood, when did they recur in adulthood? Asthma is sometimes viewed, metaphysically, as an emotional message in which your body is saying that you try to do too much to earn love from others. You don't want to admit to having limitations for fear of not being lovable. An asthma attack gives you the excuse to rest.

What similarities are there between then and now? If you develop a physical symptom:
- Where/what is the symptom you are experiencing?
- What is happening in your life now?
- Define the primary emotion that you have been experiencing lately.
- When last did you have this symptom?
- What was happening in your life then?

Our bodies and minds work together to form symptoms that act as a guideline of how we are responding to circumstances and conditions. You may notice that you keep repeating the same patterns of behaviour throughout your life; but as we learn the lessons, each repetition occurs at a higher level of consciousness and lasts for a shorter period of time. Eventually, you may find that you have come full circle and that through your conscious decisions you reach a point of stillness and peace. You learn to grow into a space of sharing without fear of loss; and you will see this reflected in your greatly improved physical health.

Career

We often choose careers based on our personality preferences. For instance, if we are analytical we would enjoy research; if we like detail, engineering would appeal. Advertising would draw in creative personality types; and those who want to make a difference in the world would gravitate towards careers in social work or careers that tackle environmental challenges. Some people follow what their family expects of them and others choose to find their own way.

What were your career choices? Possibly your initial choice was based on circumstance and you still wish to fulfill another line of work or study. Most of us have a better idea in our late twenties of what really inspires us and then feel it's too late to make the change. It's not. We simply slot into a comfortable rut and fear making the change. If you did change direction or jobs, when was this? What changed within you that motivated you to make the change in how you earned your living? You may find that you outgrew certain environments; that you had accomplished all that you needed to accomplish there.

Step by step

As we work through our obstacles, the first phase is usually dealt with by addressing the self. We go to therapy and do self-work to get all our internal stuff out there so that it can be resolved and released.

Once we have really looked at ourselves, we often move on to the next phase by treating our unresolved issues externally. We might do this by helping other people solve similar problems in their lives, or by moving to, and interacting with, new environments – and them with us.

Ideally, we should hear the messages brought to us by an environment that keeps pressing buttons; one that that reminds us of past trauma.

We should use this opportunity to come to a place of forgiveness and understanding; and as we do, we will find that the same stimuli no longer trigger the same emotional response.

Over time you may come to sense that you are finished with some insecurity or fear and you can release and detach from its grip. Once this happens, you need time to heal; open wounds are easily contaminated. You have a right and a duty to yourself to let go of what is holding you back so that you are able to sense the freedom and lightness that life has to offer, without feeling guilty for having this feeling. It is not an act of selfishness if you don't want to stay involved in other people's problems. In fact, you will be making space for someone else who needs to be where you were. By raising yourself out of your pain, you create brighter and happier memories and your presence will radiate hope to others. You will *show* them how to be.

Baggage backpack

When you discard your heavy baggage-backpack, try to resist the need to carry the baggage-backpacks of others; this is not helpful to anyone. Try to support others without an emotional pay-off, and know that what you are offering is for the betterment of all beings – including yourself. Assist others without *any* expectations. You do not have the right to deprive others of the opportunity to resolve their own issues.

When you have finished reviewing yourself you can step into bonus time. This is the time in which you actively choose what you want to do and how you would like to engage with the world. You may say, "But my life will be empty without having issues to resolve." This could cause you to create external issues just to feel alive, or safe, or normal. However, you need to see this as a new level of being – a new space of awareness – in which you will encounter different challenges. Possibly, the issues that you now deal with will be internal, such as the quality of your thoughts and your attitude towards yourself and others, and you should feel less inclined to be drawn into old patterns of unconscious behaviour. The conscious choices that you make will be focused on what you would like to do to bring to yourself feelings of joy. Keep asking yourself, "Am I really doing things that bring me joy?" And learn to sense what is good for you. Life is not necessarily a Calvinistic struggle, and you are not rewarded for self-flagellation.

We are given a short time on this Earth plane to find our hearts, to open them, and to learn to honour the beauty of the Universe. So stop looking for fear and pain – these difficulties are harder to find than love and light.

And as you look at out at the world and decide on what it is that *you* want from another, do you look at yourself and ask, "What is it that I have to offer another – without losing my relationship with myself?"

Choice and free will

Many people live unconsciously and are automatically fulfilling a role. Life becomes a stimulus and response cycle – like an amoeba under a microscope that is being prodded by rays of light. It retracts from impulses, and then sends out pseudopodia when it feels safe, only to retract yet again when fearful. Free will is the biggest dilemma most people face. It is actually our greatest gift, but we look at it in fear because it means that we are responsible for everything that happens to us, and all that has happened to us in our lives.

Some of us choose not to live life in conscious awareness, because we are not willing to take responsibility for our own decisions; nor are we willing to live with the circumstances that emerge from these decisions.

People generally like to be told what to do (although they will not admit to it) because they can blame the decision maker; nothing is their fault. Many of us are hypnotised and are essentially sleep walking. We don't even bother to find out who is holding the remote control.

How to stay brain dead

There are various ways of staying unconscious. There is alcohol, drugs, gambling, sex, and of course, work. One of the major non-addict ways is being stuck in finite belief systems that forbid us to think differently or question anything. There is a vast difference between the way things *should* be and the way things are *meant* to be. One you are told, the other you have to find out by trial and error – by experience.

How successful have you become at alienating yourself from expressing your truth, from feeling alive? Do you selectively hear and selectively remember things that suit you, to the detriment of those around you? Because we form a dynamic part of our environment, nothing that we do happens in isolation; and you may find that you are starting to receive the same treatment you are giving out to others. Are you conscious enough to realise that you created this response through your own behaviour in the first place? It is true that our thoughts create our reality, and we can change them. We are what we think. And the wheel does turn.

Some of us only wake up when we are shocked. When the power supply to the treadmill is turned off and we are forced to find our own power. This is a blessing, and these blessings come in different packages: retrenchment, divorce, death, and terminal illness.

Two options

If you are at a crossroads in your life and are unable to decide between two choices – whether about a job, a relationship, or a holiday destination – the answer to both is usually *no*. Neither is appealing or inspiring enough. The right option has yet to arrive. Take a step back and look at what is right in front of you. Or take a lateral view, and do not stay stuck in what you perceive to be your only options. It could be that this current choice merely made its appearance to awaken you to another concept; to allow you to investigate other possibilities. It brings a message, a clue to the answer, but is not always the answer in itself.

It is usually the small things that cause us the greatest amount of angst. These are minor irritations when taken in isolation, but in a swarm can be very debilitating. It is much easier to deal with major crises because they will be recognised as such by most others and therefore there are strategies to help us cope. In a crisis we become very focussed because there are no alternatives. The situation is pure and uncluttered. It *is* the small stuff that makes us sweat – not the big things.

If you surround yourself with pain, you will stay in pain. It has a resonance and it will keep your buttons alive. Value yourself, and the Universe will reward you. Make a conscious choice to be responsible for your actions and to honour and enjoy the gift of free will.

A Cherokee parable

An elder Cherokee was teaching his grandchildren about life. He said to them, "A fight is going on inside me. It is a terrible fight and it is between two wolves. One wolf represents fear, anger, envy, sorrow, regret, greed, arrogance, self pity, guilt, resentment, inferiority, lies, false pride, superiority and ego.

The other stands for joy, peace, love, hope, sharing, serenity, humility, kindness, benevolence, friendship, empathy, generosity, truth, compassion and faith. The same fight is going on inside you and inside every other person too."

The children thought for a while and then one child spoke up, "Which wolf will win?"

The Elder replied simply, "The one you feed."

Listen with *honesty* to your inner voice. If you identify with being a slut, you will become an emotional prostitute. Choose a relationship in order to relate, not in order to be dependent on another for self-construction and self-identification. Know who you are.

Learn something new; it will teach you something new about yourself. This activity takes you away from your fixations and dependencies and into other aspects of yourself. Your perception of self will change. Break the cycle of feeling like a victim and empower yourself.

DOING THINGS
DIFFERENTLY

༖

*I bring to you the message of authenticity ... when you
tell yourself the truth, you live your truth and your thoughts
will be reflected in your actions, and there will be no room
for darkness.*

༖

There is no point in getting into a relationship for selfish motives. If you resort to playing games, you will only be spiting yourself. If he goes out with his friends without taking you along, it is a reminder to you that you should make the effort to maintain your friendships. Do not go out alone to spite him. What is your intent in doing this? Do you really want to go out, or are you just going to get back at him?

Are your actions born of love or fear? Are your actions pure? Is this chosen behaviour for the highest good of yourself and others, and does it bring you happiness?

Be consistent in your behaviour. Aim to do no harm; live and love your truth.

Do not relinquish your dreams and wishes. Learn to feel and know what it is that *you* want. Remember that you have free will along with the responsibility and accountability that goes with that. Who do you wish to be now that you have freedom of choice? Find an environment that supports and expands your potential – because the spiritual path can be a lonely one – until you resonate with someone on the same frequency.

With each new relationship we vow not to choose the same sort of person or make the same mistakes within the relationship that we made in the past. But we cannot hope to achieve this unless we examine and understand certain aspects of ourselves, such as how we view commitment, and whether we are truly ready to share heartspace with another.

Commitment

As it is with all behaviour, commitment cannot happen in one realm and not in another. If we are true to ourselves, our behaviour will always be congruent over a range of activities. If a person is uncommitted in the workplace or to their family or their pet, they will be uncommitted in all their relationships. If you find yourself saying, "I'll see how this goes, maybe I'll look for a job in Dubai. I'm thinking of emigrating – there must be some better place out there," this reflects an unwillingness to commit to the moment. This is very different from dreaming or wanting to improve your life. If you are always hankering after something, you will never commit to your present circumstances since all your thoughts and energy will always be somewhere else in the future. No other place or relationship will ever be satisfying if you are not willing to put your energy into what you are involved with now. You will live a life of half-hearted attempts.

Role models

There are occasions when someone would really like to commit, but they do not have the training or role modelling to sustain a healthy commitment. For them, the idea of permanence or sharing space means unhappiness and evokes fear. The entire concept of sharing a living space with another in a committed relationship feels unsafe to such a person.

These thoughts develop over time during our growing years as we were often forced to watch hostile interactions between our parents, sometimes being caught in the middle of these disputes. We may have been cited as the problem in the house; or maybe one parent used us to gain sympathy for their unhappy situation. This type of environment is one of conditional acceptance – often there is very little love and affection, too many rules, and a lot of punishment involved.

The kind of underlying messages you may have received while 'sharing' with your parents could have been, "You are not welcome; Don't think that you can just eat and sleep here – this is not a hotel; Here we have rules and if you don't live by them, you will be punished; You have no self-identity and no rights because I own you; You are under my roof now and you'll do as I say." And all you want to do is get out of there so that you can have your own quiet, safe space.

How committed were your parents to you and to each another? Did they support your issues or were you blamed for things that were not your fault? Could you go to them for support, encouragement, and direction? If not, it will be more difficult for you to know how to commit in future interpersonal relationships because you don't know what it looks like. However, there will have been other significant connections in your life who will have shown you how to do this, but did you see it? Sometimes new information is so unfamiliar that we don't believe it and therefore choose to ignore it.

Later when you decide to move in with a relationship partner, all those old messages come back. The unconscious feeling will be that you do not have the right to your own life. You have to follow the rules and toe the line and this could make you feel suffocated. And logically, you might look at your current relationship and find no obvious flaws, and yet you feel the need to escape. You are remembering your early training and having the same knee-jerk response. It is not conscious, but your early fears are reactivated because once again you are sharing with someone on whom you feel a certain sense of reliance. It may not be financial now, but it could be emotional.

You may find yourself saying to your friends, "I'm bored," or "I'm so tired," or maybe, "I don't know what I want in my life anymore. I'm confused." It is exhausting to live in what your early programming has defined as an unsafe environment. This is a primal survival response, and you have learned that the only way to maintain your identity is not to enter the situation – or to leave. The fault lies in the fact that you are inserting an outdated template onto the situation. You are no longer living with your parents and you have the right to decide on what is good for you and how you deserve to be treated. You should maintain your identity within a committed relationship; you are not an extension of the other. It is healthy to do inspiring things for, and by yourself, as well as doing things with, and for others. Sharing with those around you is wonderful, but choose those others wisely.

Right and wrong reasons

There are both right and wrong reasons for commitment. The right reasons would be making a conscious choice – especially when you have a good relationship with yourself. When you decide to have a committed relationship, you need to feel that it is an absolute priority for you. It is something that you should value above almost everything else; otherwise it can very soon become neglected.

The need to be married or in relationship because you don't like being seen as single – or the need for someone to come home to after you've had your fun for the day – or the need to have someone on tap to feed your ego, are the wrong reasons for going into a relationship. Going into a relationship to satisfy one's insecurities is a dead end. Insecurities are highlighted in a relationship and all your fears will be realised.

It is also not advisable to become pregnant to gain a relationship since only strong, bonded relationships cope well with children.

Paths

Do people belong to each other? No. We share our paths and walk along-side each other in parallel. There is no ownership. We each have our own path and are accountable to ourselves and to our Maker. We cannot belong to, or be an extension of, another person because we are all learning to find our own way. We are all different.

To commit means that you choose to share your journey with some-one; to be both student and teacher to one another. It is a wonderful opportunity for spiritual growth and enlightenment because seldom are we tested as deeply as when we are emotionally vulnerable. Trust and respect are the two most important ingredients of any relationship. If these qualities are missing, the basic foundations are lacking and the structure will not be sound.

Look to people's actions and not their words to find out whether they are able to commit or not. If someone cannot commit to a dinner arrangement or makes great suggestions for weekends away that never materialise, they cannot commit. They are waiting for something else to happen or some other circumstance to make their decision for them. Just because someone is married does not necessarily mean that they have committed to the relationship. They could just be comfortable in the circumstance because it suits them. Always look to see whether he or she is walking their talk.

Sharing work to make the relationship work

Both partners can contribute different talents and goods to the communal pot and co-create and build a fulfilling relationship together. If we share tasks and work with one another, we will not feel taken for granted by the other. Instead of thinking, "What can I get out of this relationship?" consider what you can contribute to the relationship.

Do the things that fulfil you and that are an expression of yourself. Live your life as if you were single; but do what you do with love, not with vengeance. Both partners should maintain their self-identity and should not feel as if they are losing part of themselves by sharing who they are. Every action we take should be viewed in the context of the best possible outcome of the relationship.

Over-responsibility

Do you have an unhealthy need to control the environment; and do you find yourself taking on the responsibility for someone else's behaviour? This applies to both the work and home environments.

If you do everything yourself because only then do you feel it will be done properly, you are not giving anyone else the opportunity to try. You are taking away their responsibility. In the end, doing everything results in burn-out because everything has become your problem. Yet you wanted it that way.

Why does this happen? You could have learned as a child to take responsibility for a parent. You may have believed that if you did not, something would go wrong and your safety would be threatened. You need to learn to ask for help and to accept help when it is offered to you. Allow yourself to be nurtured and learn what that means. Stop parenting everyone – including your partner. You will not save the world, nor will you save yourself. The situation is not the same as it was when you were little. Let go of control and allow others to enjoy doing things for you as you enjoy doing things for them.

Look at whether your self-worth is invested in being seen as organised and together. What quality of life does this behaviour bring you? Is it necessary to always want to solve other people's problems, or does this help you escape your own? Are you denying someone else the opportunity to do things for themselves because you fear being made redundant, that they will no longer need you? Take some risks and be 'irresponsible'. Free yourself. Stop monitoring your partner and the environment and let people be. Don't count the number of cigarettes she smoked at the party or the number of drinks he has had. It is not your problem. Stop enabling other people's irresponsible behaviour by cleaning up their mess. Being responsible for your own life and your actions in it should keep you busy enough.

Students and teachers

Relationships are our greatest teachers and we remain students in this realm throughout our lives. We are sociable beings and our interaction with others forms the invisible web that can either be our greatest support structure or a trap. How we work with these interactions will determine how our interactions work for us.

Relationships with others are not hard work – hard work is confronting your relationship with *yourself* when you choose to be in a relationship with another. Hard work is staying conscious when you are in pain, because of the feelings you are allowing yourself to feel.

Societal norms dictate that we form conventional partnerships to have families. However, this does not mean that it is right for everybody, but it does push those who choose not to conform out onto the lonely fringes. The world is, sadly, full of judgement because those who toe the line want everyone else to toe the line for fear that someone out there may show them that they were wrong and that their way is not perfect after all.

Condense all your bad experiences into a drop of personal power – a drop of knowing and understanding of that which you will attempt not to repeat. A mistake is only a mistake if you do it again.

Everything that is around us is designed for relationships. We go out to clubs and venues to find love. We dress up to attract someone. We meet for coffee to make up or break up or to start a new relationship. The cars we drive could be 'babe catchers' and the babe we catch will have spent the afternoon being pampered and groomed somewhere in town so that you can go down to the mall and show her that ring; and so she can start talking about the house she saw yesterday.

Look at the shape you are in today and remember those who moulded you and chiselled you, how you were buffeted by the harsh reactions of some and soothed by those who cared.

All of who we are and how we respond is created by our interactions with what we relate to in our world – the loss of a pet, the birds we feed in the morning, our work colleagues and our family, as well as our chosen relationship. We are constantly shifting, changing, re-shaping and adapting to find the most comfortable fit in the world that we create.

Trust the lessons

Remember that as soon as you learn a new lesson or integrate a new *a-ha moment*, the experience will heighten. Do not be despondent; the head stuff has to be integrated into your heart – so go with the flow. For example, consider what would happen if you were to suddenly accept that your emotions should not be an extension of your partner's behaviour; that your emotional stability is a separate entity from your partner's actions. As soon as you have realised and understood your co-dependency issue, your partner will engage in behaviour that tests your understanding and acceptance of the lesson. It is not conscious – it is how the Universe teaches us. Your test is, "I am worthy being me and I am worthy both with my partner and without. Their behaviour does not upset me." Once you change and stop giving your partner all your attention and your energy, he or she may initially resent your new attitude because they are accustomed to you having a certain response. As soon as one person's behaviour changes, there will be a change in the behaviour of the other. It is as simple as that. If you want a different outcome from a situation, change your behaviour. There is a definition of insanity, apparently attributed to Einstein, which says, "Insanity is doing the same thing over and over and expecting a different result."

Priorities and types of love

A hierarchy is a means whereby we can arrange or prioritise things; it is an order, which is usually vertical. We rank many things in our lives, including our relationships. We prioritise those that we feel are important and meaningful to us and we give them more attention and care, and those that are less important to us, we neglect.

Ideally, the ranking of our relationships should be the following:
- Our primary committed relationship should be with Spirit.
- Our secondary relationship is with ourselves.
- Thirdly … our friends and our community.
- Finally, with a significant other.

We have to fulfil the first three before considering the fourth. If the first priority is last and the last is first, we will be putting all our hopes, trust and beliefs in another human being, which is an unrealistic expectation to have of anyone. Do not go looking for love; you will never find it. Find the love that exists within yourself and learn to give it to *yourself* first; and only then can you look for someone else with whom to share it.

Sternberg (Sternberg, R.J. 1986) proposes that love can be conceptualised as consisting of three primary components: passion, intimacy and commitment. These can be demonstrated as a love triangle with the three components forming the vertices, as shown in the diagram on the right.

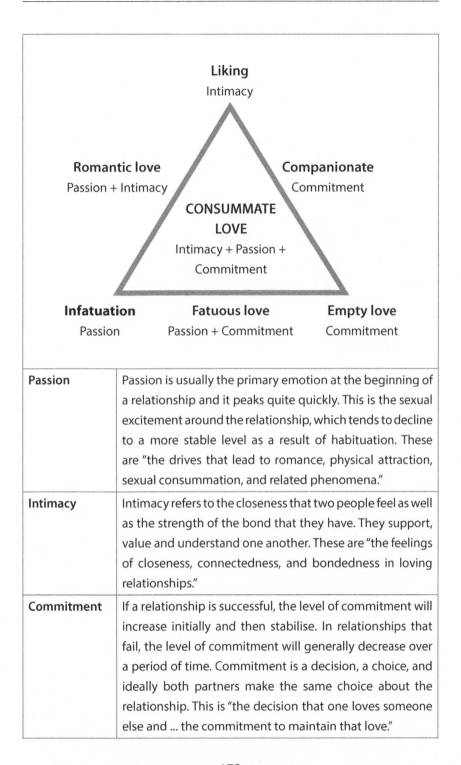

Passion	Passion is usually the primary emotion at the beginning of a relationship and it peaks quite quickly. This is the sexual excitement around the relationship, which tends to decline to a more stable level as a result of habituation. These are "the drives that lead to romance, physical attraction, sexual consummation, and related phenomena."
Intimacy	Intimacy refers to the closeness that two people feel as well as the strength of the bond that they have. They support, value and understand one another. These are "the feelings of closeness, connectedness, and bondedness in loving relationships."
Commitment	If a relationship is successful, the level of commitment will increase initially and then stabilise. In relationships that fail, the level of commitment will generally decrease over a period of time. Commitment is a decision, a choice, and ideally both partners make the same choice about the relationship. This is "the decision that one loves someone else and ... the commitment to maintain that love."

These components may be combined to characterise the eight kinds of love shown in the table below. Sternberg notes that the relative emphasis of each component changes over time as an adult romantic relationship develops.

Kind of love	Passion	Intimacy	Commitment
Non-love			
Liking Friendship without passion or long-term commitment		✓	
Infatuation Passionate and obsessive love	✓		
Empty love Decision to love without passion or intimacy			✓
Romantic love Physical and emotional attraction but no commitment	✓	✓	
Companionate love Based on common interests and friendship as well as mutual respect and concern for the other's welfare. A long-term committed friendship in which the passion has faded.		✓	✓
Shallow relationship – a whirlwind romance	✓		✓
The ideal relationship	✓	✓	✓

Sternberg, R.J. (1986) A triangular theory of love. *Psychological Review*, 93, 119–135.

We cannot change our essence, but we can change how we express it. You can change your response to another's behaviour and in so doing, you could modify a situation.

Do you spend so much time trying to change another because you do not want to look at what you need to change about yourself? And would you be happy knowing that someone is wanting to have a relationship with you because they want to change you, or would you prefer to have them want you for who you are?

Why then do you want to change another? Often it is the very thing that attracted you to them in the first place that you now want them to lose. The only outcome of this situation is that they will be less authentic with you to avoid your criticism.

Do you find that you still need to control someone else? And do you need tangible proof that this person is influenced by you, following your orders, and fulfilling your wishes? Do you want to control them because you fear something? Maybe it is just that you want to own him because you need more of his attention. In this case it might be better to invest in a pet, not a partner.

People have different qualities that they express to a greater or a lesser degree depending on which buttons are being pressed. Someone can change their overriding expression in the environment because they choose to become more of one aspect of themselves and less of another. The other traits are left to lie dormant. Changing one's behaviour requires a great deal of work and an ongoing desire to do so. The pay-off of the new behaviour has to be greater than the old one.

Being relationship ready

Sharing heart space – are you relationship-ready?

Have you had enough single time to reflect on who you are and what you want? You should have a better and more realistic idea of what type of relationship is good for you now.

What aspect of relationship do you prioritise? There must be enough points of intersection with your new relationship partner to bind you. Do you share enough common interests and enjoy doing things together? That is how we build our relationships – by sharing time doing things that we both enjoy.

Are you willing to feel vulnerable and even at times to be hurt? Are you ready for the next lesson? Once you decide to relate with your heart and not with your head, be prepared to FEEL!

Can you maintain your true identity in this new relationship? Can you be who you are without fear of rejection or loss?

Can you honestly look at this new relationship and say, "This relationship brings me joy and supports my self-worth?"

Remember that the pillars of a solid relationship are: trust, support, friendship, acceptance, and kindness. Do you feel that you will be able to uphold these with your new partner?

What do you know about this new person? What is his or her relationship history? It is a very good idea to do some investigating. Are they grounded and honest, the kind of person you may have called boring in the past? These are the real people. Be realistic and realise that you will see parts of yourself reflected in them and vice versa. It happens like that. We are human.

Our environment

How do you interact with your environment? This place is the arena in which you interact with others and the one of which you too are a part. It is your community, your society, and your work place. The microcosm of your experience will be a reflection of the macrocosm of the broader society because we are all little pieces of the same puzzle. Together we make up the bigger picture. The environment impacts on you as you impact on the environment. Nothing happens in isolation and there are always broader permutations to our behaviour.

Work environment – your second home

The thread of your early life and your current home life will run through your work environment. This becomes your new 'home' and you will usually transfer your communication training and emotional issues into this environment because there will be people there who remind you of your parents and/or your siblings. Sometimes the work environment becomes your first opportunity to rebel against your father, openly defy your mother's instructions, or to fight with your brothers and sisters. If you felt invisible or invalidated as a child, you may be desperate to prove yourself in your career to make up for not being recognised as a child. This may result in you manipulating and destroying others to get what you need. Sadly, all you want is to find your self-worth and, ironically, you will never get that from others.

Review your work history and consider whether your work choices were conscious choices or not.

- When did you start working?
- Did you leave home to earn your own money, to be independent as soon as possible?
- When you chose your job or career, was it circumstantial because your options were limited at the time?
- Are you in a work environment that supports you?
- Is this really the job that you want?
- Does it reflect who you are?
- What does it teach you about yourself?

We are only able to make conscious choices when we're awake and know why we are making them. Once we reach a greater level of awareness, the directions we take will be a brighter reflection of who we are; and we will be more able to find what it is that we want.

The breakdown of extended families and communities in modern society has resulted in a decreased amount of responsibility we feel for each other – and as a result we are encouraged to increase our competitiveness. Self-actualisation becomes self-greed and self-need and people resort to base expression – a primal action instead of a higher altruistic goal.

Is it really worthwhile doing things at the expense of others for personal gain and living *apart from*, instead of being *a part of*?

Look at the people you resent and those you respect, both at work and at home. Which family members or relationship partners do they remind you of? If you felt unsafe having an opinion as a child, it is very likely that you will suffer from unworthiness and are one of those people who never feel they can do enough at work. You will always be grateful for the salary you are getting and will try to do more – even feeling over-responsible for a bad vibe in the office. When you do find out that you have been underpaid, you will be livid because all the old resentments of not being valued will resurface. When this happens, go and *ask* for a raise. Try to assert your self-worth. If you do not value yourself, no-one else will.

Balance both worlds

Is there a balance at home and at work? Do you get as much out of your job as you put into it? Some jobs offer little money but there are great rewards on other levels. Other jobs offer lots of money and provide very little satisfaction. If there is little reward and a bad wage, you should leave.

Harassment

If you were sexualised too early as a child, or were physically and/or sexually abused, this pattern could continue into your workplace as you will not have learned how to maintain good boundaries or healthy relationship patterns.

If you had to follow excessive orders as a child, these situations may make you feel intimidated because you have learned that not following orders means punishment. You may have conditioned yourself to believe that it is easier to do what you are told than to stand up for yourself. Do not allow yourself to be subjected to abuse – and that includes abuse in any form and in any environment. If you cannot change the situation, get out. The Universe always supports the decisions that you make out of respect for yourself.

What do you do when you feel that bosses or colleagues are sexually harassing you at work? Do you know that you have the right to say no?

Corporate culture

Does the corporate culture of the company that you work for encourage honesty on all levels? Does the company really promote moral values or do the people involved have posters about moral values on their walls without ever carrying them out? Often companies send out mixed messages by promoting insecure people to senior positions because they are easy to manipulate. When others see mediocrity being rewarded, it leads to dissatisfaction and distrust because of the double standards that are implemented. How many people are willing to rock the boat when they see through the game? Are you the same person at home and at work? Or do you have different personalities? If so, you need to look at why there is that fragmentation.

Community and society

Does your community support dishonesty and betrayal? Who are the heroes and what is their behaviour? Are you in a society or community that rewards positive self-worth and healthy relationships? And do those who surround you value supportive relationships between people; or do they ostracise you for wanting to change?

If a country has a high crime rate and people feel fearful and insecure, this leads to stress that permeates all levels of society – including interpersonal relationships – because insecurity becomes the dominant thought. Hopelessness can eventually result – especially if everything appears chaotic and you feel that you have no control over those things that adversely affect you. You hear that petrol and food are going up in price, that leaders are not being punished for crimes they committed, that innocent law-abiding people have fewer rights than criminals... Ultimately, we will feel disempowered because there are no clear guidelines and most people are uncomfortable living in a grey zone. We generally prefer to have rules. They make us feel safe.

• Who are your societal role models?
• What do they do and how do they behave and market themselves?
• Why would you choose to be like them?

The more obsessive you are about creating rules and structure for yourself, the more energy you will spend creating boxes to feel safe. And then you will have to guard the boxes and cages that you built for fear that someone may take them away. You disempower yourself. However, you have the choice to buy into the voice of the herd and get sucked down by all the dysfunctional information; or to ignore the negativity and stop being indoctrinated with fear.

Re-evaluate yourself:

- In what or whom do you place your safety?
- What are your levels of trust in yourself and your environment?
- If you are religious or spiritual, why are you not respecting that this circumstance is perfect?

There is always order in the chaos and you would not be there if you were not able to find the opportunity within it.

Group thoughts

Our group consciousness permeates our way of being and triggers our own issues. An obvious example of this was Diana Spencer's funeral. We saw our life and our pain reflected in her. When she died, we as individuals grieved our losses and we all felt each other's grief. We cried for our lost emotional opportunities. She was the catalyst who encouraged us to open our hearts and to be openly expressive about our emotions.

We are not always that conscious of how we are affected (both positively and negatively) by the emotions and behaviour of others. Our thoughts are very powerful waves of energy, and the focussed thoughts of many people can cause incredible changes in the ethers. The literature on mass meditations and prayer meetings shows how conscious intent can influence the thoughts of others in an environment.

Interconnectedness

We are humans in a town in a country on a continent on planet Earth in a galaxy ... The way that we are within our world influences the environment. And the environment, in reflection, influences us. When the moon is full we feel it and when people in faraway places are devastated by floods and earthquakes, we feel for them.

It is not the country, the place, or the house that you live in that you need to change in order to find something new. When you move, you will take your baggage with you and recreate more of the same elsewhere. The all-encompassing environment that triggers positive and negative behaviour within you, and your ability to hear the messages as a result, is the only thing that really changes. What is important is how you are when you are in that space. And the behaviour you choose because of the emotions that you feel at that particular point. Your environment is your backdrop; your mirror. You take your stuff into it and it reflects your issues back at you.

No escape

There is no escaping yourself. Therefore, it does not matter where in the world you go, you will create the same issues in that new environment because you carry your 'backpack' with you. Ideally, you should know which environments best supports who you essentially are and try to surround yourself with that which supports your truth and your soul journey. Consider making your life easier by knowing what type of environment expands you and raises your levels of joy.

Living in an environment that contracts your thoughts and diminishes your self-expression can eventually chip away at your optimism and cause you to self-sabotage because you lose your ability to continue to see the incredible possibilities. If you are in an environment like this, it is up to you to use the situation to rise to the challenge of being who you really are, and meeting who you need to meet. By doing this, you can achieve incredible growth – if you are willing to step out and find yourself. Learning to read your outer reality is essential if you want to awaken to who you really are.

Have you learned to say, "This is what I choose because I am worthy?" Choose places in which you feel inspired and in which you can inspire others. Always be authentic. Your inner resonance, your personal frequency, needs to be congruent with the outer resonance otherwise you will continuously feel out of balance. Reflect the inner and the outer, and consider whether your job reflects who you are …

Relationship with animals

Animals are essentially souls in fur suits who teach us how to truly open our hearts. Why do you think your dog keeps asking you to go for a walk? He is trying to get you to get up off your couch or away from your computer and is encouraging you to change environments and get some exercise. He knows what is good for you and he accepts you unconditionally. Is your love for your partner this unconditional?

And when your cat gets under your feet, she wants you to slow down and play a while. Do not take life so seriously. Cats are also especially sensitive to energy fields and will gravitate towards someone who is ill because they want to provide them with healing. They will try to place themselves on the area that needs the most attention. They are attuned to the subtle energy of the Universe and they try to maintain balance.

Animals are not selfish and they try to teach us unselfishness through their unselfish behaviour. They model for us the reality that we are all part of an ecosystem; that we all belong to the greater co-created biodiversity of the planet. There is a place for everyone and there is always enough of everything – as long as you are not greedy or fearful. Animals teach us to treat each other with truth and compassion, and they teach us that we need to nurture the earth if we are all to survive.

Sadly, animals survive as a species only if humans find them useful; usually for material gain. Their survival is dependent on our needs and wants and yet they are so much more evolved than we are on so very many levels.

Our fur-friends know that life is simple. If something smells off, they know it and they leave it alone. Humans, however, will sit around and hypothesise about it; prodding it with philosophy and playing with it until they smell of it themselves. And once you smell of it you cannot smell it anymore because you are part of it. So animals teach us not to fudge or over-think the issues. If it smells like shit, it is shit.

Do not fraternise with the enemy. You know they are the enemy, so stop saying, "*Keep your friends close and your enemies closer.*" That is short-sighted because your enemies are saying the same thing to each other about you.

Sing like a bird when the sun comes out and find shelter when it is cold and rainy. It is good to be able to know the difference between the two. Appreciate all the little changes in your environment and be awake to the messages from the animal kingdom. They know what is good for us.

Relationship with Spirit

Why do people often respond more strongly to evidence of the Devil than to evidence of God? Do humans believe in God because they fear the Devil?

One hears the challenge, "Prove that God exists." And you hear others say, "Prove that there is no God." Proof is the basis of the rational, analytical mind. Theorems and formulas are used to define the probability of something that exists within the human paradigm. Spirit is not part of this man-made known world and should therefore not be interfaced with it. We cannot extrapolate spiritual concepts using earthly tools; Spirit lives in the creative heart space. You will feel its presence as the trees moving outside your window feel the air. Although you hear nothing, the trees still respond to the spirit of the wind, as you are moved by the breath of Spirit.

There have always been and will always be arguments around religion. Who is right and who is wrong; but is it really important? The core messages in all religions are the same – and yet we disregard the Universal Truth because of our need to be right. We will sacrifice ourselves to have our enculturation validated because if that is seen as wrong, we have to revise all the indoctrination that makes us feel safe. So we resort to your God versus my God. We divide and rule; which benefits people in power because it is easy for them to mobilise armies for territorial advantage since the people have already been divided.

The underlying message in all religions and spirituality is that you need to love your neighbour as you love yourself, and do no harm. Know yourself and be willing to share. Instead of following this basic message, we choose to kill each other in the name of peace because our self-righteous attitude and fragile understanding cannot deal with the threat of another's interpretation.

Unfortunately, most of humanity will not adopt an attitude of *both/and*. We want human rule books that define our spirituality as either this or that. Surely it is obvious that all is one? Spirit is everywhere and nowhere – the alpha and the omega; the beginning and the end; the order in the chaos. It is indefinably present. Everyone wants the same thing. Every living being sends out rainbows of hope to remind us of who we really are and where we are going; if we choose to feel and see the messengers and the messages, we will find our way Home.

If you go to a bookstore, you will find reams and reams of information on how to find yourself or how to develop your healing or psychic potential. These are all tools; they are crutches and a means to an end. You can also attend courses that will teach you techniques that involve studying and getting diplomas and getting accredited; and in the end you realise that all is connected through your heart and that life is a living meditation. You can be shown the way, but ultimately you have to put the information into practice. Once you have aligned with your inner voice and guidance and have accepted yourself as a spirit of light in a physical body, you will not need to do any further research or to search any further. You will have moved out of your head and into your heart and will be able to feel the pulse of eternity that resides there.

Shedding negative energy

All systems are held in balance and therefore goodness will be balanced with evil; and love will be balanced with fear. This is why we are given the gift of choice. We have free will to decide what we choose to see, hear, and do. The greater your level of fear, the more hate there will be in your heart. It is up to you to choose which universe you wish to subscribe to. When you are happy, good things happen to you and the world looks fine. When you are angry, everything goes wrong and the world seems dark and gloomy. Nothing has changed except your perspective. Your perspective becomes your perception of your reality.

Psychic waste bin

The irresponsible concept of putting your rubbish into a psychic waste bin is neither logical nor realistic. If you release negative energy from yourself or your environment, dumping it will simply result in someone else becoming contaminated, since energy is neither created nor destroyed. It carries on. A more efficient way of dealing with redundant issues is to transform and transmute that energy into something else by raising it to a higher level. By doing this, it will change its form, and the impact on you and others will be different.

Thoughts are energy and will remain in an environment until the vibration in that environment has been altered. Most of us feel this when we enter a room – it has either a tense or a welcoming vibe; the place gives you either an uneasy feeling or a relaxed one because you are experiencing the lingering reminder of what has happened there in the past.

Be careful of surrounding yourself with negative people. It takes unnecessary energy to neutralise their negativity, energy that could be better used elsewhere. Energy moves like invisible smoke – it will still cling to you no matter how hard you try to stop it from happening. Therefore, it is better to learn to recognise it so that you are able to avoid it in the first place.

Life's purpose

We often read about the concept that everyone is here for a purpose, that we all have a unique gift or talent that we need to find and only when we do, will our lives change from a dull and grey existence into something special. We will be recognised. Many people consult astrologers, pin-code analysers, and aura readers asking, "What is my life's purpose?"

Your ultimate purpose is to know yourself and to be yourself. Your presence is your gift to others. It is not about huge meaningful contributions to society or great works of art. It is about Spirit experiencing itself in physical reality. There's nothing to look for and nowhere to go – it is with you all the time.

Stop looking outside for love and affirmation and start loving within first. Be authentic and accept all of who you are and all of who others are. Be aware and conscious of what is happening around you, how it affects you, and how you, in turn, affect your surroundings. Broaden your scope of vision and say, "I am what I am. Now, how can I add value to myself and others by being who I am?" Our words must be followed through by our actions, otherwise they are meaningless. Your purpose is to truly love and be loved.

Wish list

The accepted Western way of drawing up a wish list and using it to visualise your perfect life as-you-want-it, and your perfect partner (as you expect them to be), contradicts the workings of Spirit. Of course you must have direction and know what it is that is good for you, but the trick is to put your wishes and hopes out there in trust; and to be completely willing to accept what is sent to you. You need to trust that Spirit knows not only what you want but what you need for your growth.

If you restrict yourself to only what you want and to what you know, your focus will be narrowed to limited opportunities. Your request will be framed by your human limitations and you will miss out on all the magical opportunities that are waiting for you. Ideally, we should truly surrender and say, "What is it that I should be doing with myself in this lifetime? I am open and ready to receive your guidance in whatever form you choose to reveal it to me."

Learning to communicate with Spirit requires total trust. If you get a feeling to do something and instantly resort to rationalising its validity, it is lost. You are meant to listen unconditionally and feel the difference between your wants and the requests from Spirit. As with everything, this takes time and practice. If you want something, ask for it – but then let it go. Be aware of the difference between essence and form. If you ask for a particular job (form) you may get it but not be happy. If you ask for a job that produces certain feelings such as one that challenges your organisational skills (essence) you leave it up to the wisdom of Spirit to set about creating such a job. And it often takes a form you would never have imagined. Be careful what you ask for, it may just happen, and sooner than you think. Remember that Spirit does not discriminate between what you ask for when you make your requests. If you spend your day rushing around saying, "I'll never finish...I'll never get this job...I am useless," it will be granted to you. Your negative affirmations become your mantra; they seem to be your wishes because you keep asking for the same thing. Anything that you fixate on by repeating it becomes a request; and that is what you will receive. Change your thoughts and be conscious that there is no separation between prayer time and daily life. Live your truth.

If you pray or ask for something thinking, "This will never come true," it probably will not materialise because you have made that doubt part of the prayer – and prayers are always answered. Why are you thinking negatively about your wish? Is it because of a lack of self-worth? Do you feel unworthy of receiving gifts from Spirit; or do you have issues of trust? Do you always need evidence of how things work? You have to believe that what you're praying for is possible, and you need to ask with the right intent, knowing that you will be given what is for your highest good. Do not try to control the outcome. If it does not happen the way you envisaged, it was not right for you for now. All will become clear in time. What you need is not necessarily the same as what you want. Trust, trust and trust; everything will be perfect. This is why we so often hear, "Thy will be done," and not "My will be done." Do not take on everything yourself when you can delegate; you are allowed to ask for help. And when you ask, say as the Wiccans do:

"For the good of all
According to the free will of all
... And so mote it be ... "

Simple rules

If something smells, it is off. Do not spend time trying to rationalise how much it smells and why. Trust your feeling about it and flush it away. Inner guidance is *the* only truth; so listen and trust and be willing to shine a light on lies and deception to uncover the truth.

Always ask yourself, "Am I living my life for me or for someone else?" Use your feelings to determine what is good or bad for you, "How does this situation feel for me?" If it feels good, do it and have fun. If not, don't go there.

Life is simple if we follow the simple rules – do *not* complicate it. Switch off all fear and open your heart. You have free will. You either listen to your inner voice or you ignore it.

The life after this one

Our world and our existence are *not* compartmentalised into two separate blocks of experience...
1. the here and now
2. the next life or heaven or whatever you choose to call it

We all evolve through different states of being – like water – which makes up roughly 75% of who we are. We live in our physical form in order for our souls to have a human experience. Our journey continues into the next state the way water turns to steam; we leave the limitations of our bodies behind. In the same way, we should not separate people into those who are here and those who are not. On a soul level, there is no distinction. You are what you are; just in a different state of being.

Someone once said, as they were passing into the next life, that they were experiencing a vision of a tapestry. They saw the underside of it full of knots and loose ends and intertwined strands of different coloured cotton threads. And as she got closer, the tapestry turned around and the full picture on the other side was perfect. It is like that. We are all interwoven in what we think is a mess, but we are actually part of a perfect creation.

And when you pass into the Spirit world, you will be greeted by what you created during your time on earth. You will be welcomed and led into the next life by the highest expression of yourself. You will not die alone – your Higher Self is there always; to remind you and to guide you to your purest angelic potential.

References

Baumrind, D. (1971). Current patterns of parental authority. *Developmental Psychology*, 4, 1–103

Bookwala, J., Frieze, I.H., & Grote, N.K. (1994). Love, aggression and satisfaction in dating relationships. *Journal of Social and Personal Relationships*, 11, 625–632.

Dion, K.K., & Dion, K.L. (1991). Psychological individualism and romantic love. *Journal of Social Behaviour and Personality*, 6, 17–33.

Hensley, W.E. (1996). The Effect of ludus love style on sexual experience. *Social Behaviour and Personality*, 24,205–212.

Sternberg, R.J. (1986) A triangular theory of love. *Psychological Review*, 93, 119–135.

Harlow, H. (1958). The nature of love. *American Psychologist*, 13, 673–685.

Maccoby, E.E., & Martin, J.A. (1983). Socialization in the context of the family: Parent-child interactions. In E.M. Hetherington (Ed.), *Handbook of child psychology: Socialization, personality and social development*. New York: Wiley

Damasio, A. (1998). Emotion in the perspective of an integrated nervous system. Brain Research Reviews 26 (1998) 83–86

Hendrick, C., & Hendrick, S.S. (1986). A theory and method of love. *Journal of Personality and Social Psychology*, 50, 392–402.

About the author

Dyan is an integrative healer and counsellor offering a variety of modalities to help promote the physical, emotional, mental and spiritual well-being of her clients.

She has a longstanding background in the medical industry as a medical technologist, doing pharmaceutical sales as well as project and laboratory management. Her interest in metaphysics began in 1988 after a near-death experience.

Vibrational healing is her passion, which includes aligning mind, body and spirit to the rhythm of life as a means to a joyful and calm way of being. She does this using reflexology, sound healing, EFT (Emotional Freedom Technique), Reiki, massage, aromatherapy, counselling, and yoga.

Dyan believes that science and spirituality are intertwined. Everything forms vibrational patterns and the key for us is to find our unique note – our inner harmony. She assists her clients to harmonize their flow to a note of joy and to live their lives 'on purpose'.

Dyan runs her healing practice in Cape Town, South Africa.

Visit www.iamdyan.co.za